RISING TO NEW LIFE: STORIES FROM MAHER

Maher (in the Marathi language) means
"Mother's Home":

A haven of hope, belonging and understanding. Maher's mission is to help destitute women, children and men from all over India exercise their right to a higher quality of life, irrespective of gender, caste, creed or religion.

Rising to New Life: Stories from Maher
Copyright 2022 by Darcy L. Cunningham
All rights reserved

For more information and to make a donation,
visit https://maherashram.org/

Back Cover photo, interfaith wedding photo, interfaith program photo, map of Maher sites: Amol Tribhuvan of Maher.

Remainder of photos from Maher files or this author.

Table of Contents

Forward from Sister Lucy 1

Introduction 5

Chapter 1: Maher's Beginnings 11

    The Dawn of Maher 11

    The Early Days 12

    Staff Begin to Join Maher 17

    Other Challenges 18

    A Haunting Story 20

    "Sister Lucy, Why Didn't You Just Give Up?" 23

Chapter 2: Women's Stories 25

    From Abuse to Independence: Aadhya's Story 25

    A Mother Works Hard for Her Children Her Whole Life: Sarah's Story 29

    Fed up! Even Well-Off families Have Abuse: Charrika's Story ... 31

    Destitute and Unable to Speak the Local Language: Dariya's Story 34

    From Homeless to Respected Professional: Ekani's Story 37

    Family Complexities, Including Prison: Gauri's Story 41

    Maher's Para-Social Work Program: Ishani's Story 44

    Support Through Nursing College: Jalsa's Story 46

    For the Sake of the Children: Kajal's Story 51

    Reunited Across 1000s of Kilometers: Lalita's Story 58

From Professional Career, to Hell, to A Whole New Life: Megha's Story 60

Always Room for One More: Nisha's Story 66

Chapter 3: Re-Marriage 71

Divorce, Though Technically Legal, is Rare: Omaja's Story 71

Remarriage After Widowhood: Prisha's Story 73

Even Older People Want the Companionship of Marriage: Sarah's Story 80

Chapter 4: Children's Stories 84

Married Too Young, Abused, Destitute By Age Sixteen: Ridhi's Story 84

Living on the Streets to Social Worker at Maher: Raksha's Story 85

Abandoned, Separated, Reunited: Two Sisters 87

Abandoned, Orphaned, Then to New Life at Maher: Triya's Story 89

Lured by Promise of Good Jobs, Forced into Prostitution: Two Sisters Tell Their Story 93

Resilience of Children: Unni and His Three Younger Siblings.... 95

Education Leads to Independence: Abhijat and His Mom 97

From Maher to Homeless Soccer World Cup Games in Chile: Mahika's Story... 99

From Desperately Poor Tribal Village to Leadership: Yadavi's Story 101

Even Sister Lucy Can't Save Everyone: Yashoda's Story 104

Abandoned: A Beautiful Boy 108

Chapter 5: Babies at Maher (Born Here or Found With Their Mother) 112

Raised by Maher staff from Birth: Zuri's Story 112

Child Born of a Child: Anika and Binita 113

Sometimes It's Tricky to Do the Best for the Child and Still Follow the Rules: Chaya's Story 116

Raising a Toddler When His Mother Is Unable: Ganga's Story 118

Chapter 6: Families 134

Tragedy Strikes: the Story of Deepa and Her Son, Raj 134

A Family Comes to Maher: the Stories of Varsha, Vikram, and Their Mother 139

Helping One Person Lifts the Generations to Come: Eshana and Her Family 144

A Father's New Beginning Lifts the Whole Family: Suyash's Story 151

Chapter 7: The Fruits of Maher 154

From "Untouchable" to Beloved "Brother" and Role Model at Maher: Mangesh's Story 155

Coming to Maher As a Child, Remaining As a Social Worker: Vinayak's Story 159

From Poverty to Finance Professional: Surekha's Story 161

A Girl-child Demonstrates Her Value and Her Gifts: Poonam's Story 163

Once an Orphan, Now a Homeowner and Trustee of Maher: Yogesh's Story 168

From Orphan to Scholarship to Degree in Psychology from U.S. University: Ravina's Story. 178

Curiosity, Talent and Determination: Amol's Story 186

Baby Girl Comes to Maher, Grows into a Maher "Ambassador": Soni's Story *192*

From Unvalued Girl-child to MSW: Padmini's Story *199*

From a Boy Washing Cars to Leader at Maher: Gaus's Story .. *200*

Chapter 8: Sister Lucy's Story 209

"How Does Sister Lucy Do What She Does?" *209*

About Interfaith and Caste *213*

Challenges, Lessons, and Wisdom *217*

Lessons from My Family *219*

"Doing the Needful" *222*

Looking to the Future *227*

Chapter 9: How You Can Help 228

Appendix One: 235

Vision, Mission and Values of Maher 235

Appendix Two: The Genius of Maher: Seven Areas of Uniqueness 237

Appendix Three: Map and List of All Maher Centers in India **Error! Bookmark not defined.**

Appendix Four: Additional Publications about Maher 242

Forward from Sister Lucy

As Maher's Founder, I am pleased to present *Rising to New Life: Stories from Maher* by Darcy Cunningham. In our first 25 years, Maher has been blessed to touch thousands of lives through our residential and outreach programs. From its inception, Maher has proactively upheld gender equality, justice, and interfaith harmony as the unshakable pillars of all our work for humanity and nature. We have made a profound difference in many lives, and these inspirational stories make these human dramas accessible. In these pages you will read of women's lives transformed, children emerging from hopelessness to lives full of promise and hope, and entire families uplifted from crippling destitution into dignified lives.

I receive many requests for more stories of Maher's people. I am eager to share these stories more widely because they inspire everyone who hears them, just as they inspired us at Maher as we witnessed these dramatic events unfold firsthand.

Rising to New Life: Stories from Maher is based on interviews with more than 300 Maher community members. These are real-life stories of people from all walks of life in India, recounting in vivid detail how they faced and overcame often insurmountable odds to transform their lives, with loving support and encouragement from the Maher community.

RISING TO NEW LIFE

Taken together these stories constitute a remarkable tribute to the power of the human spirit, and they inspire tremendous hope at a time when it is most needed in our troubled world today.

There is another even more important reason why I am pleased to share this book with you. These stories are not unique to Maher; they can happen everywhere. The need for work such as Maher needs to be carried on by people like you and I—worldwide. My hope in sharing these stories is that you are touched, stirred, even inspired to do something yourself—not only to support projects like Maher, but also to see and offer what is needed in your own communities. Let the stories in this book inspire your heart to help create similar stories in your own life and community.

I asked Darcy Cunningham to write this book because I trusted her to fulfill my vision. Darcy has been a regular visitor to Maher over the last ten years as well as a regular host to myself and other Maher travelers to the U.S. She has visited nearly all our sites across India. She wrote an earlier book about Maher: *Dignity from Despair: A Step by Step Guide for Transforming the Lives of Women and Children—Successful NGO Creation Using the Maher Model.* She understands many of the details of Indian law and culture within which Maher works.

Many of these stories I personally shared with Darcy, especially for this book. Many of our young

2

Stories from Maher

adults know Darcy well and told her their own stories directly. Maher staff and I provided clarifying details to make this book as accurate as possible. All the events described here are true. To protect privacy, we have changed the names of most of the women, children, and men who have shared their stories.

We are delighted to dedicate this volume to Maher's friends in India and around the world. Your generosity has made it possible for us to create nurturing spaces and fountains of happiness, goodness, hope, support and transformation in sixty homes in six Indian states. I hope you find joy, hope, and inspiration in this volume, reflecting a small portion of Maher's work. May this book be just a beginning, and may all of you be the continuation of many more of these wonderful stories—to nurture and transform our world.

Introduction

When Maher's founder, Sister Lucy, speaks at events around the world, or welcomes visitors to Maher, the stories she tells are compelling, especially outside India. Many of these stories have "happy endings." Some leave us hopeful that the people now have opportunities for a better life. Other stories are clearly a work in progress, especially with children still growing up.

Listening to Sister Lucy, we hear of powerful hope and of unspeakable trauma. Witnessing, and being helpless in the face of a great trauma, is what led Sister Lucy to create Maher.

Our world, not just India, is in crisis. So many people experience poverty, food insecurity, domestic violence, alcoholism and desperation. Education is disrupted or even lost. There is so much religious and caste intolerance, and blame and anger, and a loss of deep human connections. We must find new forms of responding and healing. It is my hope this book of stories might be a small contribution to this effort.

Engaging and responding requires that we not only learn about others, but that we *feel* their stories. Sister Lucy believes that we must "engage in connecting from our own heart to the hearts of others in need." More of us must step up and answer the call, in whatever ways we can.

Maybe we will even feel moved to donate to Maher to support their on-going work. Sister Lucy (and I) will be deeply grateful for this. But Sister Lucy says her heart will be touched to hear of people who take even more steps—whether in their own local communities or farther afield.

One of the best ways to connect from our hearts to the hearts of others is to know the stories of those who have come to Maher in a time of need. Some of these stories were told to me by Sister Lucy or other staff. Some of the stories were told to me by the people themselves. I have taken the liberty of editing many to first person, as they would have originally told their stories to Sister Lucy and staff. Other times I wrote from Sister Lucy's voice, as if you were listening to her tell the story. I have also included background for context and clarity. The group of young people, who grew up at Maher and are now young adults, all either told me or wrote their own story for me for this book. Most of the names of Maher residents have been changed to protect their privacy. Where needed, I added footnotes to describe Indian culture or laws that pertain to the stories.

The stories include successes plus a few that Sister Lucy calls failures. Sometimes the traumas and the resulting habits are too well entrenched; sometimes fate comes along and steals a person's opportunity to make something different of their life. Sister Lucy

Stories from Maher

doesn't want the fear of failing to stop people from trying. Even if you are inspired to pause, to notice a homeless person, to see them, to say hello, to have a conversation with them as a fellow human being—then this book has been a success. Sister Lucy says that even a tiny opening of our hearts begets more tiny openings.

How This Book Is Organized.

Each chapter is a collection of stories representative of a certain group of people: women, children, etc. Each story depicts real life challenges facing Indian people, and the often extraordinary steps taken by Maher staff to help these people, and often entire families, "rise to new life."

Some readers will want to read every single story. Others may want to read a few from each grouping. Feel free to read a few of each; you can return and read more as you like. Chapter Seven, "The Fruits of Maher", shows the longer-term impacts of Maher's work. You will read about some of the young people who came to Maher as small children and are now grown into remarkable young adults. Many are now working at Maher with Master's Degrees in Social Work, or Business, for example. Not only do they represent the "proof" of Maher's work, but they will take Maher and Sister Lucy's dream into the future.

RISING TO NEW LIFE

The final chapter is about Sister Lucy herself, inspired by my own wonder about how she came to do all she has done. How she, with no formal training, came to be so incredibly savvy in working with the culture and laws of India and the realities and poverty of village life.

I have included some photos of residents and staff, and the main Vadhu Center. These are all clustered together near the middle of the book.

A Note About Maher Operations

If you are familiar with Maher, you may want to skip this and dive right into the stories. If you are newer to Maher, below is a brief overview of Maher operations.

Maher is unlike any "orphanage" or "institution" I have ever heard of. Sister Lucy values family deeply and aims to have each child and woman feel like they have come Home, even if it is a temporary home. Each Maher "Home" unit is usually twenty to twenty-five children with two to three housemothers. A social worker oversees about three such homes, plus each has responsibilities in area villages, such as with schools, self-help groups, and a broad range of programs offered by Maher. There are several nurses on staff in the larger centers such as Pune area.

Housemothers are themselves women who have

Stories from Maher

sought refuge at Maher.[1] In addition to receiving their own healing and support, housemother is a paid job. Their role is to care for the children, cook their food, oversee schoolwork, teach and monitor good hygiene, and much more. In short, they are mothers to the children. When the children are at school, the housemothers, with staff support, gather for group discussions, education, craftwork, meditation, etc. This time is more focused on their own needs and healing.

As of this publication date, there are 40 such Homes for children in 6 states, plus another 20 Homes for men, for elderly women, and for mentally disturbed or disabled women. There are approximately 975 children, 540 women and 123 men in residence at Maher, though this number grows daily. There are roughly 78 social workers and 105 housemothers and housefathers (for the boys' homes). There are 11 administrative staff plus other roles as well, such as 15 drivers and 22 tutors and kindergarten teachers. In addition to the direct housing and support of women and children, and men, Maher does a great deal of work in villages, tribal areas, as well as other projects, which is beyond the scope of this book. (A next book is coming in 2023 to address this work.)

Maher pays not only food and lodging for all these people, but also medical care, school fees (from

---

[1] See *Women Healing Women* by Will Keepin and Cynthia Brix for more information.

preschool to University), clothing, dance and taekwondo instruction, etc. Currently Maher receives zero government support and relies 100% on donations, both from within India and from abroad.

For more information, see Appendix Two: The Genius of Maher: Seven Areas of Uniqueness.

Chapter 1: Maher's Beginnings

The Dawn of Maher

If you are familiar with Maher, you may have heard the often-told story of how the organization came to be. The story began in 1991, when Sister Lucy was a young nun living at Hope House, a small service-oriented convent within her Order. What follows is from a wonderful evening of storytelling while a group of us foreign guests listened and asked questions. This is what Sister Lucy shared.

One evening a young woman, seven months pregnant, came to the convent (Hope House) seeking help. Due to convent rules, I couldn't offer her shelter. While I believed her, it never occurred to me that just one night would make such a big difference. Later that very night, I heard screams and ran to the village. I recognized the woman, literally on fire, running towards me. Her husband had thrown kerosene on her and set her on fire. I watched helplessly as the woman and her unborn child both died a horrible death. I did manage to find a rickshaw driver who helped me take her to the hospital, but it was too late.

This event so radically affected me that I *had* to act, I *had* to create a different way to help the people around me, especially the women. Ultimately, I left structured community life (though not my Order, nor my vows) to begin Maher.

The Early Days

That first year was lonely, difficult and chaotic. I had almost no support. In fact, a lot of people expected, even hoped, that I would fail. I didn't really have a plan. I had to figure things out and made it up as I went along.

Love guided everything I did. Love was the basis for establishing Maher, so everyone who needed help was equal in my eyes, regardless of caste, class, creed or gender. Women and children deserved the same rights and education as men; God came in many guises, and all deserved to be respected; animals and the earth were God's creatures too. These convictions guided and sustained me through challenges, the unknown, adversity and even direct opposition.

I was searching for land. Sixty-seven plots of land I reviewed, but none were within my budget. I knew what I wanted: I wanted a good road, a school nearby, water, a health center nearby. I finally bought the land where the office and Aboli house is now, in Vadhu Budruk village, outside Pune. This was the only one that had all my criteria that I could afford. An Austrian man came and helped me look and gave me money to buy land. Even this narrow piece of land was more than my budget, but a few more people each gave me a little bit and that's how we paid. No one was ready to help me with finance as people were not sure what I was going to do.

Front: Maher's original building (2500 Sq Ft.) Now office space. (Vadhu Budruk village) Behind: second building for sleeping, cooking, meeting, etc. Now includes Aboli House.

I could see this area was growing, so soon I bought

the land across the street, but I kept it as it was, a jungle.[2]

Sister Noelline was very sad and upset when I told her that I wanted to move on, to live in the village, in order to do more work for women. We had worked together for nine years. We had a beautiful relationship like that of a mother and daughter. This created a lot of tension and she refused to help me with finances. I think she had a great hope that I would fail and come back to her. But the Divine had a greater plan, and I was blessed with many other friends.

Women kept coming in, bringing their children. Soon there were seventy children in this house. Can you imagine? All in one house. There was no staff besides me.

I started, and in no time, we were overflowing. Women and children, lots of children. And no money. I am out in the villages: no one here has money, only in the cities. Here they will bring me two tomatoes, two potatoes—like this they would give to me. Late in the evening I used to go to the market to pick up all the vegetables that had been thrown out after the vendors left. In the fields I would gather leftover wheat after harvest. Like that. With this I tried to feed all these people. They were hungry! They were growing children!

---

[2] This is where the big courtyard, six Homes, computer lab, guest quarters, etc. are now.

Stories from Maher

Oh my God—what a tough time we had! At least I was a good cook and knew how to make tasty food even with thrown-out vegetables.

In the early days, I used to get up at four every morning and prepare breakfast first. Then wake up these children, set them to washing up. [Lucy smiles over at Gaus, Mangesh, and others of these "boys", now grown-up young men, listening and chiming in.] They used to take so long, I tell you, to wash and dress. I would never allow them to wash their faces in the bathrooms. Everyone had one banana tree and one small bucket. Everyone had to go under their tree and wash their face. So this way the tree gets the water!

All kinds of ideas I had. For example, I had the idea that having animals here would not only provide milk and food, but also pleasure. And the children would learn to care for both animals and plants, good lessons for them.

I had a fish tank. Veronica gave me that tank with the fish. It was very nice. The children were looking at it and they broke it. And birds: we had a whole big netting hanging in the area where I sleep now. Beautiful love birds I had. Yellow, green, all colors. I used to so enjoy them. The children would go in and give the birds grains and play. One day they left the netting open. They are children you know! When I came back that day not one bird was left. Finished. That was the end of birds here! The tortoise got lost in the jungle

15

where they took it to play across the road.

The animals all came to us as various donations and gifts. The cows for example: my father and mother came to visit me on their fiftieth wedding anniversary. My father came with me to buy the cows because I don't know about cows. The cows we had for a long time. These were my father's gift, so I especially didn't want to lose those. Another woman gave me the goats. A person from the village gave me two buffalos. We used the milk for the children. Very nice. Later we shifted the cows and the buffalos to Vatsalydam. [Vatsalydam is a larger complex built later for mentally disturbed, challenged from birth and elderly women.]

When we used to go to the kitchen, the whole thing used to smell like a farmhouse. And the noise! The birds, the ducks "quack, quack, quack"—so loud! They made noise in the night also. Oh—and we had two dogs in between too. Our animal kingdom!

I was living in a crazy world! It was absolutely impractical to bring up seventy children, a few women seeking refuge, and also so many animals. I had gone crazy. When I used to finally go to bed, every nerve in my body was tired. So crazy! [Sister Lucy chuckled as she reminisced.]

"And we didn't listen!" chimed in now-grown-up Mangesh, laughing.

"I used to shout!" replied Sister Lucy, also laughing.

Ultimately, I realized I had to choose between the

Stories from Maher

children and the animals. I prayed, "What shall I do?"

That night jackals came and finished all the goats. This was so painful to see. My God! Snakes came and ate the remaining few birds. And the rabbits, so delicate, they died mostly from fear. It was still a jungle here in those days, behind us, around us, and on our land that we had not yet built on; it was totally a jungle.

Nearly all the animals were finished. I took this as a sign from God. I stopped with the animals. My dream of having a farmhouse came to an end.

Staff Begin to Join Maher

In those days Maher didn't do so much work outside, in the villages, so I was here more during the day. Then Hirabegum Mulla [Hira] and Anand Sagar came, both social workers. Anand came from the village nearby, and still lives there while working at Maher. I had no money. Hira had a Master's in Social Work [MSW], plus four other professional trainings in: counseling, Hindi pundit [so she can teach Hindi language], pharmacy, and sports. She could work anywhere. But she came here. In the city she would have earned so much more! I could only pay her 1500 rupees. Anand too! But they stood by me.

Soon a few Sisters came to help. Sister Leopoldine was a thorough disciplinarian! She was from my own convent. She set up a small office space here. She did not let the children go there because they would spoil everything. We set up a kindergarten in the front yard in a little tin shed. We had nothing. The church would not give us anything. Sister Leopoldine taught in our kindergarten during the day, then later at night she would do the accounting and paperwork. I was doing all the cooking and cleaning up, keeping everything tidy so I was late to finish. Then I would write my letters. We had only one table. That little space was office and prayer room, and our cots were there also! After ten or eleven in the evening Sister Leopold, Hira and I would sit there to talk about the day.

Other Challenges

People in the area were suspicious. One lady, an older MSW, heard of Maher, and didn't like it. She filed a complaint. She said that we were building toilets inside the house for example. We had a squat toilet, with septic tank, water tank on the roof, everything. A group of villagers came and tore it down because they said it was unhygienic to go to the bathroom inside. That was their thinking at the time; they didn't understand. We had to do a lot of work in this village. A lot of education.

You have to go slow with the people, introducing changes. So much I went through!

Children in the village had no drinking water so we built a water tank for the village. But they were not

Stories from Maher

keeping it clean so the children would get sick. Also their animals, such as the goats, got sick. So we had to teach them about hygiene practices.

In those days, I thought "Oh, God is punishing me for my disobedience." I had taken a vow of obedience and chastity and poverty. Poverty of course was no problem. [chuckles] Chastity was no problem. It was the obedience part! I thought maybe because I no longer lived in a structured religious community, I had not been fully obedient. Therefore, God was punishing me. Then I said, "Show me."

The more difficulties I came through, the more I prayed. I felt very close to the divine energy. I prayed walking, sitting, cooking, any time! I would ask for God to make it clear to me what to do next. I had no advice or anyone at all to whom I could go in those days. Now I have a few people I can ask something. Those days I wasn't known to the westerners or anyone. Even Sister Noelline, whom I counted on, she left me alone. She never forgave me for leaving her. I couldn't go to the convent. So the only person I could ask was my own family. Sometimes I would turn to them. But to call them I had to go into Pune, about two hours by rickshaw. There were no mobiles then, no landlines. It was difficult. Or writing a letter. That would take God knows how long to reach them. But talking to God, that helped me.

I used to cry a lot, too—I would soak my pillow

RISING TO NEW LIFE

sometimes! I did not know what to do: children were hungry, I was hungry. What food will I feed the children with? Uncertainty, especially about food, that was the hardest. Anything else, we could work it out. But without food—oh my God. I still feared God was punishing me for moving out from structured church activity.

Everyone—the convent, Sister Noelline—all were waiting for me to be a failure and to come back. My hard-working spirit had brought a lot of money into the convent also. So naturally they were feeling my loss. I had been running a hospital kitchen for the convent in Goa before Hope House. Then later, Sister Noelline was extremely happy with my work in her organization. She felt the loss of both me *and* all the hard work I did.

A Haunting Story

In the very early days, I was still a bit naïve about how destructive some parents could be. Sometimes I felt so helpless, especially with no available transportation. Even when Hira and Anand were there as staff, sometimes I was there all alone. This incident still haunts me. Here is what happened.

A man arrived and brought his two children to Maher, a four-year-old boy and a seven-year-old girl. He told me his wife had died of a heart attack and he couldn't care for the children. He brought a death

Stories from Maher

certificate for the mother. We kept a copy of the death certificate in the file in the office. We of course believed it, having no reason not to. Later, I discovered the death certificate was a fake; he had bribed someone to make it. That happens in India, but at that time I had no idea people would make a fake death certificate.

One day I saw the two children sitting outside the office and the little girl was sitting looking so sad, so lost she was looking. I asked her, "Beta what happened?" [Beta means "dear one".] The girl said that her brother was missing their mother.

Then the little boy said: "Do you know what my father did?"

I said, "No Beta, tell me what happened."

The boy said, in his little four-year-old boy voice, that his father and mother had a fight. He said "My father chopped off my mother's head. My father put my mother in a sack. And he took her in the field ... and he buried her in the field."

I thought, Oh my God!! I asked the girl, "Why is your brother saying this?" She said it was true. I asked the girl if she could tell me which village this was. I also asked if their father or someone had asked them not to tell?

The little girl said that yes, their father told them never to tell anyone. And she has been keeping this secret in her heart. Every now and then she would cry and cry. Now I thought I knew why.

21

Rising to New Life

I told myself I must learn the truth of this.

I called the father, but he wouldn't come. Again, I called and he wouldn't come, and again like this. Then one time he came. I asked him where was he living? I wanted to know which village, thinking then we could go and find the field and find the truth. He told me a name of a village and an address. But the death certificate said a different village and address. I was confused.

The third time he came, he gave another address. Each time a different address— where to search? So, I let him go. I told Hira that if this man came again to come and get me. I wanted to talk to him.

The next time he came, I said to him I was confused. The death certificate says your wife died of a heart attack, but someone came and they recognized the children. They told me that you murdered their mother. I didn't want to tell him it was the children because I was afraid for them.

No sooner did I say this than he picked up the two children, he didn't take their clothes or anything; he put them on his bike and raced away with them. He disappeared.

He had been very violent with me already. I was alone at Maher. Hira and Anand, the only other staff, were both out of Maher on other work. The man just took the children and left. I pleaded with him to wait. I told him he couldn't just take the children like that! He

22

Stories from Maher

needed to complete papers to take the children. He didn't even answer; he just took the children and sped off. Maher had no vehicle and I had no legal right to stop him anyway. (Unless I could prove he was a murderer but there was no way to do that.)

I never came to know where the children ended up. We took the death certificate to the hospital, but no one knew anything, confirming it was a fake and the children were telling the truth.

Even now I don't know what happened to these two children. Did he kill them? Because of course he was capable of anything and wanted to protect himself. Or did he sell them? Is he living with those children somewhere? I don't know anything. It's disturbing and heartbreaking.

"Sister Lucy, Why Didn't You Just Give Up?"

Ohh! The love of the children! And also the women! The women were coming here. That time that woman was burned to death because I could not help had entirely shaken me up. No way could I give up! That incident was enough for me to be working my entire life for people. It was really too much, what I saw and experienced that night. I don't know what words I can say, what was going on in my innermost feelings ... the guilt feeling, the sadness ... I don't know what I can say. Two people died because I had no courage to speak up and break the rules. When I was thinking of her, I was so very mad with myself.

Also, the fear I had in those days, the fear to disobey was so big. I was not supposed to be out there. As a nun, I was supposed to remain in the convent come what may. Sister Noelline didn't mind so much that I involved myself a little with these people, as long as I lived with her. The first step, breaking that rule, being there with that woman that night she died ... we are not supposed to do that. I did it because I was already involved with these people.

Now, today, I have become fearless. I do not worry about breaking any rules. Of course, I will stop anything if I learn my ways are harming someone; of course I would stop that.

Chapter 2: Women's Stories

Women come to Maher for many reasons: some with children, some with none; some deeply traumatized, some just need a boost; some need education, training, or support; some stay for a short while, others for many years. Some are even found wandering the streets. Here are a few of their stories.

Sister Lucy believes that restoration and healing for destitute, abused, or at-risk women and children includes family support. Sister Lucy and Maher go to great lengths to support re-uniting families divided by space, time and other rifts when possible.

From Abuse to Independence: Aadhya's Story

Narrated by Sister Lucy.

Several years ago, Maher held our annual holiday celebration on Christmas Eve. As usual, we prepared and served food and gave gifts to around 1,500 people. Staff were all physically and mentally drained from the full day of events, and they would need to do it all again the next day at a different site! Also, the electricity was out in the whole area in one of the frequent rolling blackouts.

Shortly before midnight, I closed the front door and sent everyone to bed. As I was preparing to get a few hours of rest before tomorrow's equally large Christmas function, I heard a knocking on the door. When I opened it, I found myself facing a pregnant woman with a three-year-old boy. The woman, named Aadhya, explained that they were running from her abusive husband, and begged me to let them stay the night. I brought them inside and asked several of the college-going girls to give the mother and child food and to make them up a bed. Wavering on the edge of exhaustion, I went to sleep with instructions not to be disturbed.

Just a few short hours later, near three in the morning, I was woken by a desperate knock on my bedroom door.

"Didi[3]! Come quickly! The woman is in labor!"

"Which woman?" I asked in half-awake confusion.

One of the girls told me that the new woman, Aadhya, was sitting in the toilet, in labor. Last night when she'd come in, everyone had been so exhausted we hadn't done a full admissions interview or paperwork, therefore we hadn't known she was so very pregnant. (As it turned out she was only seven months along.)

---

[3] Didi is a term of endearment, roughly translated as "beloved big sister" that many at Maher use for Sister Lucy.

Stories from Maher

When I rushed to the bathroom, I found that Aadhya had given birth.

The newborn baby, still connected by the umbilical cord, had slipped down into the toilet[4] and likely hit its head. Maneuvering in the tiny little bathroom without electricity, we were able to bring the baby up out of the toilet. We moved the mother and child onto the floor in front of the toilet. Aadhya was bleeding profusely, and the baby's little skull had been injured in the fall. As it was Christmas, our Maher nurse was home with her family. I had never assisted a childbirth and had no training what to do. Thankfully, though, I was supported by another Maher woman with more experience. Not having the nurse's equipment, this woman ran to the kitchen where she disinfected a knife on the gas stove. By candlelight, we used this kitchen knife to cut the umbilical cord, which we tied up with sewing thread.

By this time Sister Meena, though hard of hearing, had woken from sleep. She quickly called for the driver and then grabbed a bed sheet, which she cut in two. We wrapped the bleeding mother in one piece and the little infant in the other.

Throughout this time, Aadhya's three-year-old son, who had already witnessed his father beating his

_____

[4] This was a typical squat toilet with foot pads on either side of the basin hole, all porcelain.

mother, was howling and screaming in fear that his mother was again being harmed. Though others tried to calm him and sooth him with milk, he cried long into the early morning hours.

The driver arrived quickly. We swiftly but gently moved the mother and baby into the car. In an attempt to stem the flow of Aadhya's bleeding, we lay her down and raised her legs during the drive. It turned out that during his attack on her, Aadhya's husband had kicked her in the stomach which had set into motion the premature birth at only seven months.

As we raced to the hospital, the tiny little eyes of the injured child held my gaze strongly. I can still see those little eyes today, clear as in that moment.

Arriving at the hospital, the staff acted quickly to save the lives of the mother and child. Sadly, the little infant had suffered too much trauma and passed away five hours later. Incredibly, despite the profuse bleeding, Aadhya pulled through and made a full recovery in the days that followed.

Returning to Maher in the wee hours of the morning, I went to my room in a daze. Mysteriously my bed had no sheet. It being winter and chilly, I searched high and low until I finally understood from Sister Meena that it was *my* sheet she had torn to wrap the mother and baby for their ride to the hospital!

In fear of further abuse, Aadhya chose to remain in Maher and not pursue a legal separation from her

Stories from Maher

husband. Aadhya was already half-trained as a teacher. She and her son stayed at Maher another year, while we supported her to finish the rest of her training. Then she received a teaching job in another part of India and they left Maher to start a new life.

A Mother Works Hard for Her Children Her Whole Life: Sarah's Story
Narrated by Sarah.

I was sixty years old when I arrived at Maher. I was crying, and angry and very upset. I had not eaten and didn't know what to do. They gave me tea and breakfast first. This helped me to settle enough to tell them my story.

I was very young when I lost my parents. I was married when I was fourteen years old. I could read and write. I had a good life with my husband, but unfortunately he died when our two children, a girl and a boy, were very small.

I got a job as a maid so I could look after my two children. I worked hard with many families to support my children. I educated them both in an English-medium school.[5] When they were of age, I got the

---

[5] English-medium schools generally provide the best quality education, but are private and expensive.

RISING TO NEW LIFE

children married and I continued to work as a maid.

I went to Delhi and worked with a family from Kerala. I was very happy and they looked after me as a member of their own family. They paid me a good salary too. Whenever my son or daughter wanted money, I would send it to them.

Then this family re-located to the U.K. so I went back to my home. My son was living there with his family. But he told me that he had his mother-in-law with him already; he could not look after *two* old people. So I went to my daughter, but she said she was not able to take me in either.

I was desolate and didn't know where I should go. I went to the Church close by. The priest gave me the Maher address and sent me here.

I tried to settle in at Maher, but I was so depressed and missed my children. I was so unhappy, it was hard to do much work. I still went to Church and I would see my son there. One day he told me that he wanted to take me in, but his mother-in-law didn't want me. He didn't know what to do. I told a Maher social worker and asked for help.

The Maher social worker smiled and told me she knew just how to work with families like this. They packed my bags and took me to my son's and told me to stay quiet: they would manage the situation.

As soon as we arrived, the mother-in-law started shouting and trying to throw me out. Maher social

Stories from Maher

workers stood up to her. They reminded everyone that I had sent the money for this house.

They said "This is Sarah's house! Who are you to try to throw her out! She has more right to be here than you! How will it look if the son does not care for his own mother?"[6]

The social worker promised them that if my son doesn't take me in and treat me well, then Maher will file police reports, hire lawyers, whatever it takes! And they meant it!

I got to stay and I have settled nicely now. Maher checks in sometimes to make sure all is still well. I love being Granny to my son's two children!

Fed up! Even Well-Off families Have Abuse: Charrika's Story

Narrated by Charrika.

I was forty-five years old when I came to Maher. I was married with two grown sons. The two sons were already married by this time. I had worked hard to raise my sons and be a good wife. My husband had a good job and we were wealthy. But he abused me a lot all these years. I was finally fed up! Let them see what it is like without me. I will show them I can survive on my own. I went to Maher and told Sister Lucy my story.

---

[6] Culturally, in India a son is expected to care for his parents.

I had been married and living with my husband for twenty-four years, but he never respected me as his wife. He treated me like a servant in the house. I suffered all this in silence for the sake of our children. My husband did not let me be in touch with my people and would mentally torture me. He was clever and never did it in front of the children. It was only when the children were away at school that he would harass me. Then, when they came home in the afternoon, he would behave as if nothing had happened during the day.

I tried to describe it to Sister Lucy: how my husband would "sting me like a scorpion" and then sit quietly and pretend nothing happened. This way the children heard only my voice yelling back. Therefore, when I finally told my children, they did not believe me. Yet when my husband refused to give even a little money to the children, I am the one who fought with him to give them some money as they grew older. They never knew I stood up to him on their behalf.

At times he would tell me to go home to my parents. But then he would go there and fight with me. He once beat up my sister as she questioned him. He even took me to a psychiatric doctor and asked him to give me shock treatments! I had no idea he planned this and he never informed the children either. He did this for no reason. I believe he wanted to try to show the world that I was mentally unfit. I was never mentally

Stories from Maher

disturbed and never accepted any treatment. I tried so hard to understand what was driving my husband in all this bad behavior, even wondering if he was suffering from some illness. I could not figure him out. He was a bully.

After all this, I came to Maher. I felt I had no choice. After a few days at Maher I was even more determined! I went to Sister Lucy's room at six AM one morning and declared: "Didi: even if my sons come to take me home, I am not going back home! I want to rent a room near Maher and stay. I will work in Maher's Production unit[7] making crafts to pay my rent. I will show my husband and children I can live without the support of my husband!"

I was fed up and I wanted some respect. I vowed to support myself and to prove that I could manage just fine without them all. Even though grown up, the boys did not do anything to protect me.

---

[7] In Maher's Production Center residents stitch beautiful greeting cards, or cloth purses, make candles, simple jewelry, and other crafts. Many say that creating beautiful things with their hands and working with other women like them is soothing, and Production is an important refuge for them. Additionally, all earn some money for each piece they make which Maher deposits into each individual's bank account. The women then have savings for small personal expenditures, or even to save to buy a small shop, or home one day. Maher sells the items made here worldwide, earning money for Maher. Visitors may purchase these items at any Maher site, and most "Friends" groups in U.S. and Europe also have these items for sale.

When they heard I was at Maher, they came to see me. Perhaps they finally believed me, or perhaps they were embarrassed for people to know their mother was at Maher. At least they respected me now. They brought me home and stood up to their father. They assured me that I would be safe. So I moved back home. It is ok now.

Maher follows up by phone to be sure that I am still safe and still happy to be home. They remind me that I can always return. I also sometimes call Maher, just to chat and to say everything is fine. It helps to know someone else is looking out for me.[8]

Destitute and Unable to Speak the Local Language: Dariya's Story
Narrated by Dariya.

When I first arrived at Maher with my three children, I was exhausted, afraid, and totally destitute with nowhere left to go. I didn't really understand what was happening because I could not speak or understand the local language in Pune. I had to just trust these people. Over the years I managed to learn enough of the local Marathi language to be able to tell Sister Lucy

---

[8] Maher staff always follow up with women who return home, so everyone knows these women have continued outside support.

Stories from Maher

and staff my story.

I was born in Karnataka, a state in the southwest of India. I was the youngest child in the family. I have four older sisters and one brother. I went to a Kannada-medium school, taught in the local language of Karnataka, and studied up to the fifth standard.

When I was eleven years old, I went with my family to attend the wedding of my cousin. His wife-to-be ran away the night before the wedding. Since his wife-to-be ran away, all the relatives decided and got me married to my cousin. No more than a child myself, I had no idea what was going on. I found myself suddenly a wife and torn from my family.

After that I was forced to go live in my husband's home. I lived with him and his family for four years. Then at the age of fifteen I gave birth to a son. After that a girl was born and then one more son. All along my husband never loved me. I did my best to show my love, but it was no use. He would drink and abuse me. I lived with him for eight years with my three children but all along I suffered a lot.

Finally, I could no longer stand the abuse of my husband. I fled to my parents' house. I had tried my very best to do my duty and to not break up the family, but it was hopeless. My mother became mentally disturbed from this and other tensions in our family home. My brother, who was married with two children, did not care about me. My father worked in the field and looked after my mentally disturbed mother. My sisters were married and lived with their husbands and their children. No one could afford to keep me and my children, even if they wanted to.

I had heard of Anjuman School in Pune, so, not knowing where else to go, I travelled to Pune with my children. There I learned that Anjuman School was only for orphans and did not have a shelter home for destitute women like me. I did not want to be separated from my children, so they referred me to Maher.

After the abuse I had received in my husband's house, living in Maher was like living in heaven! In the beginning I found it very difficult to adjust to the culture of Maher, and I also had to learn the local language. I worked as a housemother, helping with the children. My children went to school, got involved in the many programs for children, and made friends. They settled quickly. Gradually I, too, adjusted. I learned Marathi and worked hard.

After a few years, Maher shifted me to Miraj House, a few hours from Pune. I was kitchen-in-charge, overseeing and cooking all the meals. I also did stitching and crafts and helped take care of the mentally disturbed women. Sister Lucy said I contributed a lot to the house.

After we had been there three years, somehow my husband came to know where I was. He began

Stories from Maher

pestering me to come back to him. I did not want to go and so I ignored him. He kept trying, so to get away from him, I moved out of Maher with my children. We took a room, and I worked to support us all. It was good to know Maher was there for me if I needed help. After a while, I decided to move back to my parent's home to care for them as they were aging and ailing.

From Homeless to Respected Professional: Ekani's Story
Narrated by Sister Lucy.

Originally from Kerala and well-educated, Ekani came to Pune to interview for a job. While in Pune she met a man, they fell in love and got married. They had two children, a girl and then a boy. Ekani was a full-time mother; working mothers are still uncommon in India. However, it turned out that the man was a womanizer. He was cheating on her a lot. She told me she bore it for a long time because her family didn't approve of the marriage and so had cut her off.

Her husband had been going around with another woman for some time. Finally, Ekani accused him of cheating with this woman, but he denied it and continued. Then this other woman had a child by Ekani's husband. That was the final straw for Ekani.

She went to her in-laws and told them everything. They knew about his ways and didn't blame her. They agreed to take her in, with her two children. But they didn't really know what to do and couldn't afford to support her and the children. She had no place else to turn. She had no job, no other family to help. She felt she was all on her own.

She consulted a lawyer. He told her she didn't need to get a divorce unless she wanted to remarry. He told her about Maher, and that they would care for her and her children. Her in-laws understood and agreed.

Ekani said it was a big challenge to adjust to living in a big institution like Maher. She tried her best. She worked as housemother, learning about the care of children and how to run a small Home in the Maher way. Her children continued their education and joined all the Maher extracurricular activities.

After a few years, Maher was preparing to open a new Center for women and girls in Kerala.[9] I asked Ekani if she would like to move there to work and run this new Center. Ekani said yes, just as I hoped she would. Secretly I was wanting to reconnect her with both her parents and her in-laws, for the children's sake. I firmly believe that all children should know their families, and in India that includes grandparents,

---

[9] Previously the Home Maher "inherited" in Kerala was for only boys; after age six boys and girls must be housed totally separately per Kerala state rules. This left me in the awful position of having to turn away girls, even if we admitted their brothers. Therefore building this new Home for women and girls was a big priority.

Stories from Maher

aunties, uncles and all. I suspected that if Ekani were to return with her skills and important job at Maher, her family would come around.

Ekani and her children moved to Kerala. This was in part possible because both the children were already bi-lingual; they had learned Marathi in Pune and Malayalam, the Kerala local language, as both were spoken at home with their parents.

To start, I sent Mini down to help organize things and train Ekani in her expanded role. Mini was from Kerala too and had run the Vadhu main center, so had a lot of experience to share. The Maher Home for boys was on land next door, also with seasoned staff for further mentoring support. Now Ekani is working at this new Kerala Center in charge of the women's projects, and the girls' project, and the running of the different Homes. It is a very big job.

Once in Kerala again, Ekani was able to re-unite with her birth family and maintained good terms with her husband's family too, just as I hoped. Her birth family, seeing her status, seeing her children doing so well, came to respect her and reconciled with her.

Today Ekani and her children are all doing well. Her daughter has completed her engineering degree and recently got a job in Bangalore. Her son is completing his higher education. Ekani is proud of her children, especially her daughter with her degree and new job. She had despaired for her children when she first came to Maher with nothing. Now they are both doing very well.

Ekani expresses satisfaction and joy running this Kerala Project Home perfectly. She has built wonderful skills at Maher. She can resolve disputes between children, and with families of the women and children of Maher. She has been through so much herself, so she understands many of the feelings of others and she can come from the heart, helping other families reunite. And when reunion isn't possible, she can guide the women to take charge of their lives and their children so they can all have bright futures.[10]

This kind of success is not only wonderful for Ekani, her children, and for Maher, it also warms my heart!

---

[10] To westerners, the idea of choosing to return to an abusive husband or family seems astonishing. In India, women deeply identify with their roles as wives and mothers. Most marriages are arranged and there is no expectation of romance. If the abuse can stop and the home is safe, then many want to return. Maher brokers these returns: they negotiate dowry issues, threaten public exposure to abusive husbands or in-laws, or engage with police on the woman's behalf, for example. Maher has grown very savvy and creative in these reunions. They check on the women regularly and make sure everyone knows she can return to Maher in a heartbeat.

Stories from Maher

Family Complexities, Including Prison: Gauri's Story
Narrated by Gauri.

My mother died when I was small; my father remarried. I had one brother who is much younger. I studied up to the ninth standard. After that my father got me married.

I lived with my husband for five years, but he was an alcoholic and he used to take drugs. He would beat me up and also beat up the children. When things got particularly bad, I would leave my husband and go and live in the village for a time. Finally, when I came to know that he was living with other women, I never went back. Since I had no food to feed the children, I thought to put them in an orphanage I heard about in Kondhva, near Pune. With the children, I made it to the Pune railway station but had no money to travel the rest of the way. A policeman gave me Rs. 100 and we got to Kondhva. However, when we arrived, we found there was no orphanage there so the children and I lived in the nearby temple for five days.

A woman saw us living there and told me about Maher. She even offered to bring us to Maher's main center in Vadhu village, otherwise about two hours by rickshaw from Pune. I gratefully accepted. This woman took us near Maher but did not come inside. I am guessing that she was afraid that if Maher did not take us all in, then how would she herself care for us? So she left us near Maher and went away.

I arrived at Maher with my three children: ages ten, six, and four. When I first arrived, I was afraid and uncertain. I wondered: what if Maher did not accept me and my three children? What would I do? I only shared this much of my story because I was afraid Maher would turn me out if they knew the rest.

When I arrived, I was not well. I thought I had cancer of the uterus because my belly hurt so badly. They took me to the hospital to be evaluated right away. I was relieved to learn there was no cancer, only stress and malnutrition. They explained that I was sick from all the stress and fear I had been living with plus no proper food. The pain in my stomach was real, but it was because I was weak, near starving.

When I recovered, I worked at Maher as a housemother, cooking and caring for the children. My three children pursued their education plus joined all the extracurricular activities at Maher. One is going to college now, the other two are in school and studying hard. They are all doing so well!

After several years, when I came to fully trust Maher's staff, I told them the rest of my story.

I was on the street because my husband was in prison with a sentence of many years. Nobody could support me when he went to prison. My mother-in-law was very old; the home was broken up. My husband's

Stories from Maher

brother was also there but he was also very poor. I had nowhere to go. When I thought I had cancer and would die soon, I worried for my children after I was gone. This was really why I came to Maher.

Once Maher learned my husband was in prison, the social workers helped me follow his case. Every month, when my husband's case showed on the board, I had to go to the courts to see to his case. He was in jail in Mumbai so that is where I had to go, a good four hours by jeep one way. Then the government shifted him to Kolvapur a long way from Pune and hard for me to travel there. My far-away relatives have helped some, following the case.

Recently, after ten years at Maher, the house where our family lived in Mumbai (a tin hut really) was taken over temporarily by the government. The government people promised to re-build a group of these slum area huts to make them more livable for the people. They gave the people who lived there some money so they could rent somewhere else while the re-building happened. Only my mother-in-law was living there by this time.

Maher allowed me to bring my mother-in-law to Sukh Sandhya, Maher's Home for Elderly Women, to live during construction; there was no one else to care for her anymore. I took the money from the government and divided it up between my children and put it into their bank accounts.[11]

Then six months ago my husband was released from prison. He is now in Mumbai, staying here and there. He came to Maher to see the children. When the re-built house in the Mumbai slum is ready, my mother-in-law and husband will stay together there in Mumbai.

The children and I may go back to live with them in Mumbai when the house is ready. The children would have to change to schools in Mumbai. The whole family would be reunited then. But I am unsure how safe it will be for me and the children. We will see! It is a blessing to know Maher will help us whatever we do.

Maher's Para-Social Work Program: Ishani's Story
Narrated by Sister Lucy.

Ishani was a widow. Soon after her husband died, the in-laws put her and the three children out on the street and locked the doors. She went to her birth parents, but they too said no, and sent Ishani and the three girls away. Her own mother told her to go sit at the railway

---

[11] Maher starts bank accounts for all the children, just like with the women.

Stories from Maher

station (and beg).[12]

Ishani only had a basic education: she had completed tenth standard. She didn't know how to find a job. She heard about Maher and came here with her three girls. She was weeping because she had no place to go. We took her in with all three daughters.

At first Ishani worked as a housemother and did very well. I could see she was bright and learned quickly. I suggested she do Maher's para-social work training program, a one-year course. Ishani completed this successfully. Then I gave her work at Maher as a social worker, a more prestigious and better paying job than housemother.

Meanwhile, Ishani's three children were all at Maher. They took part in all that Maher has to offer: school, dance, sports, and more. They all adjusted very well and flourished.

Eventually Ishani's in-laws and her family heard that she was working at Maher and had a good job. Once Ishani was doing well she was no longer a burden to them. They wanted to see her and the children. In the beginning, when they invited her to visit, she didn't

---

[12] Culturally in India, once married, the woman becomes the responsibility of the husband's family. When neither the in-laws nor her birth family would or could care for her and the three children, she had no place else to go. This is common among poor families – they often simply cannot afford to feed more people. There is no government welfare or assistance in India.

want anything to do with them. They had turned her out.

I counseled Ishani to do this for her children. I pointed out that the children needed a place to go for school and religious holidays. They needed to experience family life, to know what it is like to live in a family home. I urged Ishani to maintain a good relationship with these people, even if they had treated her badly. I counseled forgiveness for the children's sake. Ishani took my advice and let her own resentments go.

The first time Ishani went to visit her in-laws, I gave her saris and gifts to take to them so that they welcomed her even more nicely. Slowly the relationship built and is going well now.

Ishani chose not to remarry. She has been at Maher fifteen or seventeen years. She enjoys her work and is doing well. Both she and the children can go stay with family for holidays.

Support Through Nursing College: Jalsa's Story
Narrated by Sister Lucy.

Jalsa Shaik first came to Maher very fed up with beatings and harassment. She told me "Now I will not go back even for the funeral of my husband!"

Stories from Maher

Jalsa was three years old when she and her sisters were sent to Anjuman Islam Boarding (a home for destitute children). She had an elder sister who was five and a younger sister who was two years old. She said while the rules were very strict and she was not very happy at this Boarding, she at least got her education.

When Jalsa was eighteen years old, she was given in marriage to Faahim Abdou. She was very unhappy in her husband's house. Her mother-in-law was mean to her, and she thought her husband was mentally ill. He beat her up often, and for silly reasons. Since she had nowhere to go, she stayed with them and eventually three children were born, all girls.

Jalsa said she cooked all the meals and did all the housework for all ten people in the household, but her mother-in-law never appreciated anything. Jalsa also looked after a cow and goats and then would go to the field to work some more. She had never done any field work before as she was brought up in a boarding school, but she learned and did her best. Still, her mother-in-law treated her poorly. Jalsa was very sad and lonely.

The family was very poor and there was very little food in the house. Her mother-in-law never gave Jalsa proper food; she only gave her food when she was in a good mood. Jalsa said very often she would steal a chapati or two to soften her hunger. Since her husband's salary was very small, Jalsa suggested to her husband that they should move to Pune where he could get a better job. For this her husband beat her up. She continued staying with them as she did not know where else to go.

One day Jalsa ran away and went to her elder sister's house, but her sister was married and also poor so she could not keep her. Jalsa's husband and in-laws made up stories that she ran away with a man, so her sister's husband did not want her there.

With nowhere else to go, Jalsa came to Maher alone. She said she left the children with her husband so he would know how much work it was to care for the house, the in-laws and the children. And she had no rights to the children either, according to Indian law.

She worked for two or three years as a housemother, cooking and caring for children. She settled well. During this time her husband married another woman, since Muslims can have more than one wife. They had one child, then she left him. Jalsa came to know the other wife had left and her husband wanted Jalsa to come back. She missed her children, so she returned home.

Again, her husband beat her. Again, she left and returned to Maher. This time she brought her youngest child (a girl) with her. Jalsa explained that years before she used to speak a little freely to a man who was her neighbor, so her husband suspected that she had

Stories from Maher

been in a relationship with that man. He beat her up badly then, too. He told her he did not believe this youngest girl child was his and declared he would not keep her.

Jalsa was very sad and upset when she returned to Maher. I asked Jalsa what she wanted to do with her life, her future and her children. Jalsa said she wanted to train to be a nurse. She thought that then she could work and support herself and even her children. So we shifted her to Pune to Prem Sagar House to be near the nursing college. Jalsa still worked at Maher as a housemother a bit, in the mornings and evenings on either side of her school day. She earned some spending money for bus fare to travel to classes. During this time Maher continued to provide all housing, food, basic clothing, and school fees for her and for her daughter.

After one and a half years she got her nursing certificate. She worked as a nurse in Maher for two years. For big holidays, such as Divali, she brought her other two children to Maher to stay with her. They cried when it was time to return home and pleaded with Mommy to come home. They said they missed her and that Granny made them do all the work. In between, her husband called a lot and they talked.

After a few visits like this with the children, she felt she needed to quit her work at Maher and return to care for her children. She waited until March after the school year ended and then they all went home.

For the last year she has been with her husband, children, and in-laws. It's ok now. She works as a nurse at a local hospital. They have come to respect her. Even the third child is now accepted in the family. We still hear from her sometimes. And she knows she can always come back if need be.

A group of women residents.

Stories from Maher

For the Sake of the Children: Kajal's Story
Narrated by Sister Lucy.

Kajal came to us many years ago as a Muslim woman from the South of India. Her family got her married to a Muslim man from Kolkata. They had two children, one girl and one boy.

After the birth of their second child, her husband got married a second time. After this he started harassing Kajal. She left with her two children and went back to her people. But they would not take her with two children. She did not know what to do. Someone told her about Maher and so she came here.

She was with us for many years, working as a housemother. The children went to school and grew up. Then the boy started giving troubles. He told his mother he wanted to leave Maher and live outside. He wanted to have a mobile phone, play computer games, and other things which Maher did not allow. Kajal said no.

When he was about seventeen years old, he ran away. For a while we did not know where he was. Then we learned through social media that he was in Mumbai. We called him back to Maher. He didn't come. So we took a Maher vehicle and went to Mumbai. We managed to find him and brought him back to Maher.

Then he told me he wanted a job outside Maher. I

RISING TO NEW LIFE

said ok, when you are eighteen years old. So when he was eighteen he took a job outside Maher.

Naturally, living in Maher, he was innocent of how it was outside, how people would use him and cheat him. He joined some trouble-making boys and they broke into a company. He was identified on the security cameras and so the police caught him. The man who hired the boys to do this break-in was not caught; only the boys were arrested. This man let the boys take the rap. There was a court case.

Maher of course tried to help him. We said he is young and innocent. We explained that he didn't understand what he was doing, he only saw the money he was offered. He didn't understand the consequences. We managed to get him out of prison on bail. Eventually we got the charges against him dropped.

Kajal was not a great housemother. She was overly strict to the girls and not very nice. I had to keep shifting her from house to house because the girls didn't like her. Her own daughter told me she felt like she was in jail. She told me "I cannot breathe when my mother is there." I and other staff argued with Kajal to try to get her to soften up some, but to no avail.

About this time, the son asked to go live with his father. So Kajal agreed and invited her husband to come to Pune for a time to all live together. The son begged his father to come, telling him his children

Stories from Maher

needed him. He came, leaving the second wife in Kolkata, about two days journey by train.

I worried that Kajal wasn't ready for suddenly living outside Maher with the whole family and it would not end well. I counseled Kajal to go slow. But Kajal left. They all lived outside Maher for this time as a family.

Soon Kajal was back seeking shelter. Since Kajal had no other options, I took her back though with misgivings. I wondered if perhaps I am sometimes too compassionate? Of course, Kajal also had the son and daughter with her. The father returned to Kolkata. The two young people had completed twelfth standard, and the boy had his B.S. However neither of them yet had any professional training—so how would they support themselves well? So there really was not much choice, was there?

Still the daughter was not able to get along with the mother. Then the daughter snuck out and had an affair with a Hindu boy. Kajal found out and beat her up. Kajal went to the boy's family and said we are Muslims—keep the boy away.

Kajal put the daughter in a Muslim institution. They expected this girl to wear the face covering, to worship only Allah, and to say the Islam prayers, which she did not know. She was supposed to have learned all that from the Koran. But this girl had been raised since she was small in Maher's interfaith environment. All religions are welcomed equally; no one is required to follow any strictures of any single faith if they don't want to. She was a very happy child at Maher. At this new place she became very, very sick. After a year and a half, the organization feared she would die so they asked for her to be removed.

Kajal brought her back to Maher. But she was afraid her daughter would again meet up with that Hindu boy. Kajal asked me to put the girl in another Maher center in a different district. Since the girl was nineteen years old now, legally I could do that. I shifted her to Maher's Satara center, about eight hours away by bus.

The daughter however was still longing for the Hindu boy. So one day she ran away from Maher and her school. She returned to Pune area and went to this boy's home. She learned the boy's parents had gotten him married and his wife was pregnant.

Now she did not know what to do, where to go. She felt and looked a bit lost and forlorn. A man, not a good man, came up to her, pretending to help. He took her to somewhere far away and raped her. She was so sad, she did not fight back.

Finally, she phoned her mother because she was afraid. She had left the house where he kept her, but she didn't know how to get back to Maher. The man had kept her near one Temple, so that allowed us to find her. Hira, Kajal and the brother, all went to bring her home. It was about a fifteen-hour journey by car.

Maher in the meantime had been looking

Stories from Maher

everywhere for this girl. When we could not find her, we filed a missing person case with the police in Satara, where she was living when she fled.

In India, when a girl or woman is a run-away from an institution, the girl must go straight to the police when found. The police then keep the girl/woman in custody in a special "women's cell" for observation and questioning. Why did you run? Where did you go? Where have you been? Questions like that. Even though she is an adult, because Maher is an institution, they have to be sure that the girl was not being mistreated at the institution. Therefore staff had to take the daughter to the police in Satara.

When the girl was found, only then did we learn that she had been raped. My focus immediately was to get this girl home from the police quickly and see to her care. To do so, we had to get them to close the missing person case first. This is not so simple in this kind of situation in India.

Kajal meanwhile was very angry; she was focused on making a police case against the man who took and raped her daughter. I counseled Kajal to go slow and think about what will happen. The story will be in the newspaper, your whole family will be named, including your daughter's name. I tried to help Kajal slow down and think about this and do it wisely. Attend first to your daughter's needs, I advised.

When I did not react immediately to Kajal's demand

to make a case against the man, Kajal was so angry she ran from Maher. The girl was still at the police station. We did not know what happened to Kajal—did she go commit suicide? I was so angry with Kajal and could not understand her. It seemed so clear that first we must have that missing person case closed and free the daughter from custody. The daughter needed to be home with her mother and family and cared for; then we could see to the other. What was the mother thinking? Why did she run away?

Additionally complicating was that the police in Satara don't know Maher very well. In Pune area, the police know Maher well and the daughter would not have been detained and questioned. In fact, the Satara police called the Pune police and learned about Maher. They ultimately released the girl more quickly than usual, though this still took several days. This also meant we were able to keep the whole story out of the newspaper, protecting the girl's reputation.

Meanwhile, when the police tried to call Kajal about her daughter, we had to make excuses like "she isn't feeling well" to cover for her being missing. When the daughter was released, we brought her home to Maher Pune.

Eventually Kajal came back here as well. She was still angry at me and did not want to stay at Maher. So she left, taking all her belongings, her money, and this time taking her son and her daughter with her. She

Stories from Maher

never once thanked me for all Maher had done for them.

This was the last we saw of her, though we came to know Kajal had taken a room somewhere in another section of Pune. We learned all three were working, which is good. But it was so frustrating too; the boy and girl could both have had good careers. Maher did everything for her and for her children, so especially her children would have a better life. It is hard when there is no thanks or gratitude, only anger. I felt like Maher did so much for this family, such as the children's education and the boy's court case. This was a lot of time, resources, worry, etc. for Maher.

I want to include this story because it is one of my "failures" and I want people to know sometimes things don't work out. They are not as happy as I would wish, but the three of them are living together and working. They are safe and healthy. Perhaps Kajal herself will always remain bitter, but I pray that her children at least have a chance to make something better of their lives.

Reunited Across 1000s of Kilometers: Lalita's Story
Narrated by Sister Lucy.

Lalita was wandering in the street without any shelter and was mentally disturbed. She was wearing torn clothes and fully dirty. One of Maher's social workers found her and brought her to our Sukh Sandhya Home for elderly women.

When she arrived, staff were unable to understand her language; they were unsure even what language it was. Sukrani was very wild and it was hard to control her. She was given a bath, clean clothes, and some food. She had full medical and psychological exams, as is standard for all new arrivals.[13] She was started on medication.

Lalita was at Maher for several years before she quieted enough to stabilize, learn some Marathi and finally remember her life before the streets. She said she was from Bengal. She began to remember her home and her family. She could finally tell the social

---

[13] All new arrivals to Maher, adults as well as children, are taken for medical evaluation to nearby facilities. This is required by government licensing bodies. Psychological evaluations are also done as needed. Maher pays for these evaluations, including any care or medicine required. Some facilities do provide discounted rates to Maher.

Stories from Maher

workers about her life, her family and where she thought she had lived.

Two Maher social workers took Lalita to Bengal, almost 2000 kilometers across India. On trips like these, we need to send two social workers, one woman plus one man, for security. One, or even two, women travelling alone on a journey is risky, hence the male social worker. The expense of this adds up.

After two days of walking and searching they found her home with three children: two sons and a daughter. All were well-educated and teachers.

Everyone was happy and crying and hugging each other. They had been searching for their mother for eight years! It was such a happy reunion! It is so satisfying when we can reunite families like this![14]

---

[14] Such stories of lost family members is sadly common in India, something people in the West can barely conceive of. Between all the language differences, lack of any centralized government services or even identification programs, plus barely any support services for stranded people, it is easy for people to get lost, be abused, become afraid, sick, or confused. All this combines to make it difficult to find lost family members.

RISING TO NEW LIFE

From Professional Career, to Hell, to
A Whole New Life: Megha's Story
Narrated by Sister Lucy.

Another organization first brought Megha to Maher. They had noticed a woman and her baby boy living on the streets; they asked to bring the woman and her child to Maher. We welcomed them both. As usual, we took both mother and child for medical evaluation. Megha at first seemed very mentally disturbed so we had her evaluated and started her on treatment. We had no idea of her history, why she was mentally disturbed, nor why she and her baby were on the streets. It took almost one year to stabilize her and begin to learn her story.

I asked her to explain what happened and how she came to be on the streets. The first surprise was that Megha was a lawyer! This is rare for a woman to be a lawyer in India.

While she was working as a lawyer, a criminal was brought to her as a client. She was working under a senior lawyer and he assigned her the case. The man she was to defend was a hired killer for politicians and rich people. She lost her case and the man went to jail.

While she was listening to this man's stories, she came to sympathize with him. Megha is a very tender-hearted person and so she was suffering that she put him into jail. She started to visit him in jail. She fell in

Stories from Maher

love with him. Then she fought for him to go free and won the case; he got out of jail. She decided to marry this man.

Even his parents told her not to marry him, warning her that he was a bad man. Her family also told her she should not marry this man. She went against all this. She had so much empathy for this man. She married him. He in turn promised he would no longer take work as a hired killer.

This only lasted a few months, then he went back to killing. Of course, this earns lots of money. He threw big parties, with lots of food. Megha said she felt she was eating the blood of the people he killed. She suffered greatly with these thoughts. She couldn't talk him into stopping. She fell into depression and then became more and more mentally disturbed. She left the house and took their baby. They lived on the streets. Both her family and her in-laws had washed their hands of her. She was alone.

This is how she was found and brought to Maher. While she was at Maher, she got better again. She said then that she felt strong enough to go back and live with him again.

I counseled her not to do that. But Megha managed to phone him and tell him she was in Maher and that I wouldn't send her home to him.

This man is a killer! And he came to Maher to kill me!

He came together with a jeep-full of other goons,

Rising to New Life

nine or so. He was shouting and accusing me. He was very drunk. They all had weapons: guns and pipes.

I didn't know what to say. So I put my arm around him and invited him to come sit, have tea, and discuss this. I explained why Megha went mad and why it wasn't good for her to live with him. I made him understand. We all drank tea together.

They wanted to argue with me, but I stayed with my "love language." I never spoke rudely to them. This took about three hours in all. After this, the goons understood. They said they only came because he paid them. They decided to leave and asked me to let the man stay and keep talking to him. They left with the jeep.

After much more talking, he felt he needed to repent for what he had been doing. I allowed him to stay at Maher for a few days for more reflection. This was a big risk keeping a murderer with us in the house. He could get irritated and anything could happen. I said a lot of prayers and sent good vibrations to him. Of course, he was alone in a room, not with other people.

Then I sent him for a ten-day Vipassana meditation retreat for which I hoped he was ready. I thought maybe he would run away from there. But he stayed. He came to understand his mistakes thoroughly. When he came back, he promised me that if I would keep him at Maher, he would not return to the work he had been doing.

Stories from Maher

I truly believed him and was ready to keep him. But my Board of Trustees said no. The risk to the other children and women is too great. They were firm that I could not keep him.[15]

Megha did not want to send him back. I did not want to either, but I felt I must adhere to the guidance of Maher's Board of Trustees. Additionally, if the government came to know I had kept a murderer at Maher, and if he did something wrong, I too could go to jail. And Maher would come to a standstill and most likely be finished. So I said goodbye to him. Megha and the boy remained at Maher.

Even with his new understanding and intentions, as soon as he was back home, he started getting phone calls. People wanted to hire him again to kill. He now could see that it mattered how he earned his money. He was truly repenting. He could not figure out to manage both the good he thought of doing and the killing work he was doing. He was in and out of jail. We don't know all the details. But then one day he hanged himself.

When Megha learned he died, she went home to do last rites with her son.[16] Maher sent them both home, along with another woman from Maher for support. At first Megha did not know how he died. Only when they

---

[15] This was before Maher had a Home for men.
[16] In Hindu culture the son is supposed to set the fire that will burn the body.

Rising to New Life

arrived did they learn it was not a natural death, that he had hanged himself. They even showed Megha a photo of him hanging! The other woman phoned to tell me this.

They conducted the funeral rites, and then the other woman returned to Maher. Megha and her son stayed on at the house.

After this we didn't hear from Megha for a while, so we didn't know what was happening with her. We couldn't reach her by phone. Finally, I sent a social worker to make the five-hour trip to check on her. Megha was not there and the house was closed up. None of the neighbors knew where she had gone. We thought maybe Megha had gotten a job somewhere.

Then one day someone called and said there is a woman who looks so familiar as if she is from Maher. But she is nude and on the street with a small boy. We didn't know who it could be and went there to see if we could help.

It was Megha and she was again fully mentally disturbed. The boy was with her. He was about four or five years old now. We admitted both, cleaned them up, and took her to the hospital. She was mentally and physically ill. They clearly had not been eating; both were thin and miserable looking. She ran away from the hospital with the IV still in her. Fortunately, she came back to Maher. She was dancing and dancing in the office. Clearly mad. We put her back in the hospital

Stories from Maher

but with more security to be sure she didn't run away again. Slowly she got better, mentally and physically.

When she came back to Maher and had settled, she said she wanted to go back to work as a lawyer. I advised her not to do that. I told Megha that being a criminal lawyer caused her too much stress. I warned that similar cases will come, she will be affected and not know what to do and then end up back here.

Megha said she still wanted to work. She asked what could she do? Then she had the idea to do a Master's in Social Work (MSW). Since she already had a law degree, she could enroll directly in an MSW program. Maher supported her to do the master's level schooling for this. She got good marks. In the meantime, we enrolled Megha's son in an English-medium school so he would get a good education too.

Megha earned her MSW degree and is now a social worker for Maher in another village. This is a big role, supporting both the Maher Homes there plus the village social worker role as well.[17] She is still on some medication, but she is managing this complex role well. However, when severe problems arise another social worker handles these.

Now her son is nineteen and doing university courses. He has been to the U.S. twice already. Both are doing well.

---

[17] This includes the Self-Help Groups and many other village programs.

RISING TO NEW LIFE

Always Room for One More:
Nisha's Story

In India there are millions of unnamed women (and men and children) on the streets. Sometimes they are ignored, sometimes offered food, often beaten, raped and taken advantage of. Only a few get help. When Maher staff see a woman looking lost and abandoned, they usually stop to offer assistance. Not all are willing to be helped in this way, but the lucky ones come to Maher. Below is the story of one such encounter, as witnessed by this author.

Sister Lucy, three staff and three western guests— including me—were driving from Pune to the Maher center in Ratnagiri (and from there to two other centers in Satara and in Miraj). We were tightly packed in the car. Some even had supplies for the various Maher centers, including a big metal wash basin, on their laps for this five-hour drive. Sister Lucy was regaling us with stories of Maher.

Suddenly the car braked and pulled to the side of the road. Balu, our Maher driver, jumped out and hurried back toward a woman on the shoulder of the road. He asked her to wait. He clearly startled her, and at first she was wary of him. Sister Lucy climbed out to walk along the shoulder to meet her, wearing her big, beautiful, Sister Lucy smile.

We looked back: the woman was wearing a reddish-

Stories from Maher

pink sari blouse. What remained of her sari was wrapped like a short "longhi" that a male field laborer might wear, leaving her legs totally bare. Her hair was tied back. Later the woman told us that when she saw Sister Lucy walking towards her, she thought: "Oh this woman is so happy she must be safe!" It didn't take more than about ten minutes before the woman agreed to come with us.

Sister Lucy put her shawl down on the front seat and shared the seat with our new friend. The woman chattered happily about having many clothes at home. She said she came from Mumbai. She said home was nearby. (We were up in the mountains west of Mumbai by several hours.) She said all sorts of things that we were pretty sure were not true.

"She has quite an imagination!" laughed Sister Lucy.

Later we stopped for a bathroom and water break. Sister Lucy gave the woman the shawl to wrap as a sort of skirt. Then we re-arranged people and goods and our guest went to sit in the back-back with Hira and Mangesh. She settled in and was mostly quiet for the rest of the trip, about one and a half hours more.

We arrived in Ratnagiri and went to Maher's Home there for destitute, aged and disturbed women.[18] We had called ahead to say we were bringing this woman

---

[18] There are four homes in Ratnagiri, including Maher's only home for those with AIDS. All but one are clustered together.

with us, so the staff was expecting her. They welcomed her, gave her a bath, clean clothes, food, and helped her to settle. We still didn't know her name or age or anything about her.

She came to sit with us after her bath and food. Sister Lucy talked a little more to her as Meera put a de-lousing medicine in her hair and then combed and braided it. Meera is the social worker in charge for all the Ratnagiri homes and has been with Maher for many years. Meera's touch and demeanor was that of a mother lovingly attending to her daughter's hair. The woman seemed to enjoy this. Once this was done, the woman got up to walk away with staff. As she walked, she smacked her hands together, rubbed them, smacked them together again a few times, while muttering softly. Mangesh explained she was "releasing anger." This was a good sign. She was still mostly cheerful, though seemingly bemused about where she was and how she got here.

The next morning she was still ok. Later that day they took her to the doctor for a health check-up and assessment. Sister Lucy said she believed the woman would adjust fairly easily. When she settled in, staff hoped to learn more about who she is, where she came from, and what happened to her.

Six months later I called to ask how she was doing. Staff updated me.

Stories from Maher

The woman has at least been able to remember her name: Nisha. She is doing well and she always looks very cheerful. She can take a bath by herself and feed herself now, too. The staff has to keep a close eye on her however because she will wander off if the gate is left open. Perhaps this is how she originally got lost? She is loved by everyone as she is very joyful and charming.

Staff are hopeful that as she continues to stabilize and heal, she will remember where she comes from. They might be able to re-unite her with her family, as has been done for many others like her.

At Maher there is always room for one more.

While we were still driving, Mangesh had posted a couple of photos to Facebook of Sister Lucy talking to the woman on the roadside, saying we picked her up. Immediately there was a reply on Facebook: "If you don't have money, why did you pick up this woman?"

Sister Lucy told us that when she sees someone like this woman "it is because God opened my eyes to see her, now, specifically, and so I have faith He will also open up someone's heart to give us the money to care for her. If the money would not come, then I would not have seen her, or she would have refused to come with us."

Staff told us more about picking up people from the roadside, a regular Maher occurrence. This time, it was

Rising to New Life

relatively easy to convince the woman to come along with us in the car to Maher. This is not always true!

Mangesh told of a time when they were trying to convince a man to come with them and he refused. As they gave up, Sister Lucy said, "We are not to be blessed with his company."

Chapter 3: Re-Marriage

Divorce, Though Technically Legal, Is Rare: Omaja's Story

Sister Lucy narrated this story, beginning with this note about divorce in India.

This story is an example of some of the obstacles we have to work through—including securing a divorce—in order to create a happy wedded ending. It is especially hard for a woman to actually get a divorce; the Indian court system sides strongly with the men. The man, and even his family, can be shamed for becoming divorced, so they fight it. Yet without a divorce a woman may not remarry, regardless of her religion.

Omaja came to Maher because her husband and in-laws were treating her badly. Her in-laws claimed that she could not bear children. She knew there was nothing wrong with her and it was not her fault. However, her in-laws continued to treat her poorly.

The real issue was that her husband was in love with another woman. He had two children with her and was keeping her somewhere else. His parents didn't know

Rising to New Life

about this. They believed that it was Omaja's fault that she could not get pregnant. The real problem was that he was not sleeping with Omaja! The husband would spend the evening with this other woman, have sex with her, and then come back to the house very late and sleep with Omaja, but of course he only slept there. This went on for nearly five years.

The in-laws still did not know all this, so finally they threw her out of the house.

Omaja had no options. She couldn't go back to her family because she knew that her brothers would not be able to marry if their married sister was living at home. So she came to Maher.

I asked her what she wanted to do. Omaja said she wanted a divorce from him so she could remarry. So that became our plan.

We fought for her in the courts. He did not agree to the divorce because he wanted Omaja in the house to be a servant. Also, he didn't want other people to know he had a mistress.

Omaja managed to be successful in this only because of the proof she had. She gathered photographs of him, this woman, and even their children. Her friends knew he was cheating on her, so they took photos and sent them to her. One of her friends' children and his children with the mistress were in the same school. So they managed to get these children's details: their school class, their surname,

Stories from Maher

etc.

Finally, we managed to get the divorce and also some compensation from the husband. It took seven years in the courts to get the divorce. Justice can take a lot of hard work!

All this time Omaja worked as a housemother. She was a very nice woman. After the divorce, we began to look for a man for her to marry. Then finally a good man came here looking for a wife. I saw he was a teacher, and very understanding. We arranged her marriage.

I was so hoping she would have children. Omaja conceived soon after the marriage and now she has a son. This proved she could bear children. The years of suffering she went through to get her divorce was really so much. She comes often to Maher with her son and her husband to see us. Now everything is settled with her and she is very, very happy.

Remarriage After Widowhood:
Prisha's Story

Prisha told much of this story, then Sister Lucy narrated what went on behind the scenes.

My name is Prisha. I was raised in the Catholic faith. I had four small children when my husband died. The eldest child was nine, the youngest only four. First my in-laws and then my birth family said they were too poor to take me with four children. We soon had no

RISING TO NEW LIFE

food in the house. People from our village advised me to go to Maher with my four children.

We went to Maher. We all were miserable and the children were already so thin when we arrived. Maher admitted all of us and looked after us. The children attended school and joined all the wonderful extra Maher activities for children. I worked as a housemother, helping to care for a group of children. Some of my children had to live with other housemothers because after a certain age, boys and girls cannot live together. I was sad and missed our life as a family. Sometimes, for holidays, Sister Lucy would keep me and all four children all in one house so I could concentrate on my children and feel us as a family again.

This helped, and my children were all doing well, but still I longed for a home life and a husband. After about eight years like this at Maher, I told Sister Lucy that I would really like to remarry. I knew she arranged marriages for some of the women. My first marriage was arranged, as is customary in India. But culturally widows are not supposed to remarry so I had no one to do this for me except Sister Lucy. I did not expect a love match. I told her I would accept whomever she felt would be a good husband.

Sister Lucy explained that at Maher they get many men who come looking for suitable brides. She would do her best. I could tell she understood my longing for

Stories from Maher

a home and husband. She sympathized too with my pain from not even being able to go for holidays with family because no one would take me with four children. I was hopeful that she could find me a good husband.

Behind the scenes with Sister Lucy:

I was shocked when Prisha first asked me. With four children who will marry her? This could be a big problem to find such a man, but I kept on giving Prisha hope. I prayed to the Divine to help find a suitable man. I felt Prisha's pain and longing.

One day I was in the office and a phone call came from another nun. She told me a man came who is interested to marry a woman. She said she would send him over for me to meet.

The man came and met with me. I learned that he was a Catholic and he worked in a restaurant. I asked him why he was not already married. He said he was one of only two children. The parents died so there was no one to help him find a partner, to arrange a marriage. He did not know how to fall in love and get married.

I listened more. He was in his early forties. I told him I did not have women his age who wanted to get married. Then I told him that there was this one woman, close to his age, and she had four children.

He looked at me, smiled, and said that he loved

children!

I decided this was promising and took the next step. I told him to come first to meet with the woman. I told him that if that went well, he could meet the children next. I wanted to let the man and Prisha meet and talk first.

Prisha continued:

Often in India the bride doesn't meet the groom until the wedding. Sister Lucy, however, felt that since I had already been married once and was no young innocent girl, I should meet this man and be part of the decision in choosing. Sister Lucy said if that went well, then he could meet the children. I had four children and I wanted them to be treated well, so it was good she wanted the man to know the children. She wanted this marriage to have a good chance of working for everyone. I felt very comfortable with this.

After the first meeting between the man and I, Sister Lucy asked me what I thought. The man seemed nice enough, and Sister Lucy seemed to approve of him. He had a job, he was Catholic like me, and he liked children. I said I wanted to proceed. He told Sister Lucy he did too.

The next step was for him to meet my children and for them to meet him. Sister Lucy advised us to spend some real time together. She suggested we all go on an outing somewhere for an afternoon together. We

Stories from Maher

could all interact with each other and see how it felt. We had to wait awhile to schedule this until he had holiday time.

She also advised me not to tell anyone in Maher about this. I only told people that he is some distant cousin of mine and that he wanted to see me and the children. This protected my reputation. This also protected Maher's reputation: it would have been a big scandal for Maher that Sister Lucy was putting women with men to meet! We agreed that since I had four children who were all going with me, I would be safe.

We went out two or three times like that. After that he told me he would like us to marry. I agreed. Sister Lucy said she was so happy for us! Maher began to plan for the wedding.

I thought it would be simple after that. I felt that since neither of us had family we could just get married. Sister Lucy counselled us that we should try to get my parents and my in-laws to come to the wedding. She explained that she wanted the children to know their grandparents. Also, if either family found out after the fact, they might start telling stories that I ran away with a man, and spoil my name. My husband-to-be and I agreed to accept her wisdom. I could not imagine how she would get everyone to agree, but we left this challenge with Sister Lucy.

Behind the scenes again with Sister Lucy:

Getting the families all to agree was a big challenge!

First I informed both the in-laws and Prisha's parents and invited them all for the wedding.

The in-laws, the children's grandparents, came to Maher. They said this isn't good; the children will be ill-treated. I pointed out that if they were really thinking of the children then why didn't they come to see them for the eight years Prisha and the children have been at Maher? They did not come even once! I told them this was not their real concern. Let them be.

And then Prisha's father came and said he would not come for the marriage. He even said I was doing things that are wrong in arranging for a widow to remarry. He was also upset that even though the boy is a Catholic, he belonged to a higher caste than she does, and that this too was wrong. Further the man is from a different state; he claimed it was wrong to marry someone from a different state. I pointed out that they have a common language, they can both talk in Hindi and Marathi. These were all the objections. Prisha's father was very angry with me!

I knew that this kind of thing takes a lot of patience, diplomacy and time, over multiple visits. I went back to the father several times to explain and work on him so that after the marriage Prisha would be treated nicely by both the in-laws and her own family. In those days I did not have so many Homes to pay attention to, so I had more time to do all this. The families kept saying

Stories from Maher

"No! No! No, we will not come! This is all rubbish what you are doing!"

I went to their village and spoke a lot with them, to help them understand. They said, "Suppose that man won't treat the children well?" I reassured them, saying that the children will stay in Maher for a while. I reassured them the children will be safe.

I implored them to think of Prisha—she needs companionship. They were not able to understand this. There is such a strong cultural objection to a widow remarrying. "Once a widow, always a widow." Finally, they understood. I managed to bring everyone around and they all came to the wedding.

Prisha continued:

Both my parents and my in-laws came to the wedding. They seemed to wish me well. I was surprised and grateful. It was a very nice marriage.

Sister Lucy did not send the children with us immediately. She knew we needed some quiet time just the two of us to get to know one another. So the children continued living at Maher. Of course I missed my children, but I knew they were all doing well at Maher. We went to Maher often to visit, to take the children for outings, and for special occasions. Over this first year, my husband and I got to know each other, to even love each other. He is respectful of me.

I found a job, plus I had my savings from when I

worked at Maher. So with my husband's job we did very well. We settled into a good marriage. After one year, we asked to have the children come live with us as a family. By this time, the children also wanted to come live with us.

The children adjusted well to our new life as a family. But they are all teenagers now and so things happen. We still sometimes call Sister Lucy for advice. She helps us understand and sort through questions and problems when we call. Sister Lucy is still connected to our family, like a beloved auntie.

Even Older People Want
the Companionship of Marriage:
Sarah's Story
Narrated by Sister Lucy.

We found Sarah on the streets: almost naked, fully mentally disturbed, starving, hair matted, sores in her mouth and on her lips. She was near death. People would give her food, but no medicine or a place to stay. Sister Agnes and I found her and brought her home to Maher. We took her to the doctor right away. Slowly, slowly we were able to nurse her back to health. I remember we had to spoon feed her, give medicine, and daily massage to restore her health.

Sarah was very ill at first, so it was only later, as she slowly regained her health, that she could tell us her

Stories from Maher

story. She didn't remember much, but she thought she was from Bangalore. We searched for family but could not find anyone. She had some education in English: in fact she spoke in English when she told us what she remembered of her life. She also knew how to do things: care for clothing, set the table, and other household matters. These observations told us she must have come from a well-off family. We guessed she was about thirty-six when she came to us, about eighteen years ago. But that is all we ever learned of her history; we do not know how she ended up on the street. It's likely she was once married, but no one knows.

Once she was healthy, Sarah was ready for a job. Maher has a placement service helping women get good domestic jobs (housework). So we found her a position with a nice family as a servant. While they were nice, Sarah missed Maher so much that she begged to come back. It is hard to always find space at Maher so the more who stay, the fewer we can rescue. But what can we do? Of course we allowed her to come back.

Sarah became a housemother, cooking and caring for children. She received a salary and could buy her own bangles and special clothes she liked.[19] She told me several times she wanted to marry.

---

[19] Maher provides most clothing in addition to housing, food, medical care and salary.

At one point she met a man at Maher. He had also been found on the street about ten years before, mentally ill, and "simple." He was put there by his family who did not want to care for him. After some time at Maher he was ok. He had never married before and he too longed to marry. He was about sixteen years older than Sarah.

At their request, I arranged the marriage which was held at Maher. Sarah had a lovely wedding sari and ceremony. Sarah was especially happy that she could now wear the traditional Marathi necklace with black beads and gold charms that all the married women wear.

After the wedding, the couple moved to Ratnagiri Center's Home for Women to live and work. They live here now as a married couple. Sarah enjoys fussing over her husband. Recently, when he got sick, Sarah tenderly bathed him and cared for him. Now he is well again.

Recently, while this author was visiting Ratnagiri with Sister Lucy, I met both Sarah and her husband. This is when Sister Lucy told me their story. Below are my observations added to the story above.

Sarah has a sweet child-like innocence, and medication that helps her. She is very, very happy. She and her husband clearly love each other and are very sweet together. They told us that they have "purpose" now in their lives at Maher. They are happy to be working. When asked if they wanted a holiday, they said no. He told Sister Lucy, "God has given me everything now because of you. Because of Maher I am alive; otherwise I would have died long ago."

Sadly, less than one year after this, he had a sudden heart attack and died. Sarah had lived with him, with joy and love, for over six years. Living without him in Ratnagiri was making her very depressed, so Sister Lucy shifted her to Nellore, to the new Andhra Pradesh project. Now she is again happy.

Chapter 4: Children's Stories

Married Too Young, Abused, Destitute By Age Sixteen: Ridhi's Story

Nanapette Children's Home brought Ridhi, and her younger sister Shruthi, to Maher because they found Ridhi difficult to handle and thought she would do better at Maher. Ridhi was crying bitterly when Sister Lucy sat with her to learn her story. Below is what Ridhi shared, plus a later update.

When I was growing up, my father and mother fought constantly. A neighbor, Madhu, helped when my mother was in the hospital one time. When I was nine years old, this neighbor lady took me to Agra and married me to a twenty-seven-year-old man. My mother allowed this probably because she felt she owed Madhu. The man likely paid Madhu for me. I didn't know this at the time. I was too young to understand any of this.

My husband beat me and mistreated me. It was awful. I was very sad and in great pain. I finally ran away from my husband and returned home to see my

Stories from Maher

mother. When I got there, my mother was gone.

My father raped me repeatedly. He said he did this because my mother ran away. When neighbors learned of the situation, they took me to the police. My younger sister, Shruthi, and I were sent to Nanapette Girl's Home. After some time, this place brought us to Maher.

I am sixteen years old now and studying in the eighth standard. My younger sister is in the same standard. Once I was married, I was no longer allowed to go to school so I have to catch up.

I long to see my parents but I do not want to live with them. I have an Auntie who I believe lives in Vadgaonsheri, in Pune. Iwant to meet her. I don't remember either my Auntie's name or her address. Sister Lucy promised to do her best to help find her.

In the meantime, Maher is supporting my sister and I fully. I feel safe and happy to continue school. I am hopeful.

Living on the Streets to Social Worker at Maher: Raksha's Story

Narrated by Sister Lucy.

A non-Maher social worker brought Raksha to Maher in 2010 when she was ten to twelve years old. The social worker had found her on the street weeping. Taking pity on the child, the social worker took her to

RISING TO NEW LIFE

her own house. The social worker knew that she was taking a risk by keeping the girl at her home[20], so she brought the girl to Maher. We admitted the child.

I spoke to Raksha and slowly learned her story. Raksha said that her mother and father were alcoholics. Then her father died, and her mother remarried. Then her mother sent her to another family, so Raksha believed her mother did not want her. That family beat her up, so she ran away and went to stay with another family. They welcomed her but made her do so much work that her hands bled, and she was in lot of pain.

One day she ran away from that house. She sat at a bus stop crying from hunger. A man and a lady saw her, gave her some food and took her to their home. The couple was very good to her, but they had a young son who used her sexually. He told her not to tell anyone; if she told, he threatened to tell his parents and said they would throw her out of the house. She was terrified. She kept it all to herself, but the boy was using her whenever they were alone in the house. Raksha hated him and she said she hated all men. She had a lot of hatred and anger towards everyone.

I noticed that Raksha would startle and look around wildly if anyone would pass by. She was very vigilant

---

[20] The risk is from the CWC, Child Welfare Committee, a government body; she could lose her social worker's license and even be arrested.

Stories from Maher

and did not know if she could trust anyone. She would get irritated with the slightest things. At first Raksha was also suspicious of me and the other Maher staff, thinking we were not good people. She received regular counseling, education and encouragement. We all began to see that Raksha was gradually coming out of her trauma—though we know this takes time.

Now Raksha is studying in the first year of a bachelor's degree program. After this she wants to go to graduate school for her MSW so she can work at Maher as a social worker.

Abandoned, Separated, Reunited: Two Sisters
Narrated by Sister Lucy.

The police brought Saira, a three-year-old girl, to Maher. They had no information about her background. We welcomed her but had no clue where she was from or how she came to be alone on the street.

Six months later, one of the Maher nurses told me that there was a small girl lying in the government hospital and no family came to see her. This nurse used to take some fruits and biscuits from Maher and share it with the little girl, Rajata.

Rajata, who was about six years old, told our nurse that she was playing on the roadside when a car ran over her and broke her leg. The doctors did everything to reset her thigh bone which had been crushed. They put her in a cast with temporary rods and pins to help the bone stabilize and heal. She could have gone home, but she had nowhere to go. The hospital staff asked if Maher could take her in. They brought Rajata to Maher with all her documents and we admitted her.

One day Saira was playing outside the office in the small playground there. Rajata, in her wheelchair, noticed this little girl and she started crying and shouting: "My sister! My sister!" Saira only stared at her.

It took us a while to understand Rajata and why she was crying so much. Rajata was unable to get up and hug her sister because of her leg. Saira was frightened to go to Rajata as she could see the pins and rods sticking out of her leg. Saira started crying with fear.

We went back to our records to see where the police had found Saira. It was written: Shikrapur. Then we looked into Rajata's file. Her hospital record showed that Rajata also came from Shikrapur. They must be sisters indeed!

We calmed Saira's fears and re-connected the two sisters. Rajata explained to me that their parents had set them down under a tree and told them to play. Their parents never came back. While the two girls lived under this tree, they would go to the roadside in search of food. One day while they were playing, a car ran over Rajata. This is how her thigh bone was broken. A man

Stories from Maher

passing by noticed the child crying and took her to the hospital where they admitted her. He had no clue that this little girl had a sister and little six-year-old Rajata was in such severe pain she did not think of her little sister. That is how the two sisters got separated. When Rajata was well enough, we went back to the village in Shikrapur to search for the children's parents, but we never were able to learn anything.

In Maher both sisters are now going to school. We encourage them to take part in dance, taekwondo and other activities. They are growing up very sweetly. Rajata, now in ninth standard, would like to be a professional dancer and social worker. Saira, now in eighth standard, has not decided, but continues with her dance practice and is serious with her studies. Both girls have a strong desire to find their parents, though to this date we have been unable to learn anything more about who their family might be.

Abandoned, Orphaned, Then to
New Life at Maher:
Triya's story

Triya and her two younger siblings, a boy and a girl, came to Maher when the orphanage in which they were living closed. When Triya was older, she was able to tell us their story.

We three children lived with our parents in Pandarpur.

My father died when I was very small. Then my mother fell in love with another man and went away with him for some time. I can't remember how long. I begged for food for myself and my siblings. We slept under a tree. We had only the clothes we were wearing. We never had a bath because we had no other clothes to change into.

After some time, our mother returned. We were very happy to have her back with us. A few days after our mother's return, she fell ill and went into the hospital. After some days our mother died. Before her death, my mother spoke to me and told me to look after my younger brother and sister. Again, the three of us lived under a tree, and I begged for food and looked after us all.

One day a doctor from the hospital where our mother died saw us living under the tree, so he took us to a local orphanage. After two years this organization closed for some reason. From there, the three of us were brought to Pune to another orphanage and from there, to Maher. We all settled and attended school and other Maher programs. I believe I was eleven years old by this time.

When I first came to Maher, I had a lot to learn. When the housemother first told me to sweep the house, I did not know how to do it because I had never lived in a home. I did not even know how to hold a broom. It was difficult to wash my clothes as I had

Stories from Maher

never done this before. I had to learn everything.

I was very happy in both the other institutions, but I like Maher the best. In Maher I feel like I am in my own house. Everyone looked after me and my sister and brother, especially Lucy Didi. When I am with Lucy Didi, I am so very happy because I feel very much loved.

I like going to school, and I enjoy the extracurricular activities offered at Maher. My favorites are dance, drawing and singing. I want to be the very best I can be to make my beloved Lucy Didi proud of me; I do not want to ever disappoint Lucy Didi.

And from Sister Lucy: After a few years, Maher staff managed to find an uncle and learned his address. I believe all children, even orphans, should have the experience of living in a family home, if possible. One of our social workers talked to the uncle and he agreed to have the three children come for a visit during a holiday time. After two days there, the children returned to Maher. The uncle stopped returning Maher's calls and wanted nothing to do with the children. We had no idea why, or if something happened. The children did not say anything went wrong.

Triya's story continues:

I completed twelfth standard and enrolled in college. After the first year I failed the year-end exams in three subjects. I took a year to study so I could retake my college first-year exams. Meanwhile I took computer training. I also began teaching dance in the Shikrapur schools and earned money for this. I also worked in the Production Center to earn some extra money. I studied hard and I passed my first-year exams. Now I am in the second year of college studies. After that I will graduate with a degree in the arts. I am very good in dance, both Bollywood and Kathak (a classical Indian dance).[21]

My brother is in twelfth standard studying to become a journalist. He enjoys singing. My younger sister, is in eighth standard. She has a harder time in school than my brother or I did. We are all grateful for Maher's support and that we could all stay together.

---

[21] Kathak, the word itself means storytelling; it is the dance form in which the artist tells the story through song, music along with incredibly intricate movements of feet, hands and facial expressions. This dance form was originally created to tell mythological stories in temples, in the Northern states of India. It is the only dance form which has incorporated the values and traditions of both Hindu and Muslim cultures and also uses Urdu poetry and verses in the performance.

Stories from Maher

Lured by Promise of Good Jobs, Forced into Prostitution: Two Sisters Tell Their Story

My younger sister and I were born in Assam, a state in Eastern India. We lived there with our family. Our family was poor, so my sister and I needed to find jobs. My sister was fourteen years old, and I was fifteen years old at this time.

A man came to our village and promised us good jobs in Mumbai with a well-paid salary. He took us from the village to another man, was paid and disappeared. This second man brought us to Mumbai and handed us over to another man. He also took money and disappeared. We were frightened but could not get away. This next man brought us to Pune and sold us to a woman who ran a brothel.

The brothel owner dressed us up like prostitutes. We were very uncomfortable and even more frightened. We were put in two separate rooms in the same building. One day the police pretended that they were raiding the house. Then the policemen, in uniform, raped us. We were locked up in this building and raped repeatedly over nine months.

One day there was a real raid. This time the brothel owner took all of us girls to a nearby temple to hide. While we were all in the temple, my sister and I managed to get away to a rickshaw. We asked to go to the railway station because we remembered we came here by train. We wanted to go home. While we were looking around not knowing what to do next, the railway police stopped us. We were very afraid they would take us back to the brothel, but they did not. The Pune railway station police brought us to Maher.

Maher cared for us. They gave us food, normal clothing, shelter, and so much patience and love. Slowly we began to recover. When we felt safe enough to talk, we told our story. Sister Lucy asked us what we wanted to do now. My sister and I agreed that we wanted to go back home to our family in Assam.

We told Maher the name of our village and what we could recall about where it was. After some work, Maher found our family. Two social workers from Maher traveled with us to take us back to our home so we would feel safe on the journey. We were so happy to be reunited with our family! Our parents were happy to have us home again.

Closing note: often families refuse to accept the girls back because they are no longer virgins, even though the girls are not at fault. Thankfully this story had a happy ending.

Stories from Maher

Resilience of Children:
Unni and His Three Younger Siblings
Narrated by Sister Lucy.

A kind woman, Mary, brought these four children to Maher in 2015. She told me how she came to know these children and what she had learned of the family's situation.

A few days before, the children's mother, Anjali, had come to see Mary, bringing all four of her children. She pleaded with Mary to give them all shelter. She said that her husband was an alcoholic and was abusing her. Sadly, Mary did not feel she could help them, so she sent them away. She was also unsure how true or immediate the danger was, as India has many such stories.

A few days later this mother, Anjali, was murdered by her husband. The eldest son, only six years old, was witness to the murder. After killing the mother, the father got frightened and ran away, leaving the four small children on their own.

This eldest boy, carrying the baby girl, led his siblings the three kilometers back to Mary's office. The children had overheard the conversation between their mother and Mary. Miraculously, this six-year-old boy remembered the way to her office. They told her what happened and asked her for help. Mary said all four children were very tired, hungry and dirty. They were so tired that they slept in her office. She also gave them some food. Mary was totally amazed that they had walked all that way to come and meet her on their own.

Before she took any action, Mary went to visit the children's home to learn more about their situation. She met the people of the slum and met the old grandfather of the children. He was too old and too poor to care for the children. These children had nowhere to go and no one to take care of them. It was very upsetting. Mary phoned Maher and told us what happened. We asked her to bring the children to Maher right away.

Little Amaya, the one-year-old baby, was so weak and sick when she arrived that she had to go immediately to the hospital. She remained in the hospital for fifteen days. Her immune system was very weak; she needed treatments and vitamins. Maher paid for all this. Then we brought her to Vadhu Center where her siblings were. We kept all four children together at first. Only the eldest two had begun to go to school so we enrolled them locally where they could walk to school with other Maher children.

When the next two younger children, first little Manu and later Amaya, were old enough to go to school we shifted these two to Pune so they could begin first

Stories from Maher

standard in an English-medium school.[22] We enrolled these two in the same school so they would be together.

Now (about five years after their arrival at Maher) they are all in school and doing very well. They are adapting to their new life. The father was caught and is in prison. We try to support the family bonds of these children. Our social workers take them sometimes to visit their grandfather who is still living in the slum. Also, we bring the two smaller children in Pune back to Vadhu Center whenever there is a holiday or program, so all four can be together.

Education Leads to Independence:
Abhijat and His Mom
Abhijat wrote his story for Maher.

I came to Maher in 2003 at about age five. My family was very poor. My father passed away when I was small. After this, my mother was unable to support us on her own and neither her family nor her in-laws could

---

[22] English-medium schools are all private and offer children the most opportunities in India. However, a child can only enroll in first standard; they cannot transfer from a government school later because they won't be able to keep up in English. Whenever possible, Maher enrolls the youngsters in English-medium schools, and even English-medium kindergartens, even though these are more expensive. These schools are in Pune, or other cities, and not out in Vadhu or other small villages.

RISING TO NEW LIFE

afford to help. With no other options, she came to Maher with my three-year-old sister and me.

We settled at Maher and I started school. When my little sister was old enough, she began school also. I was always good in both academics and sports. I had a keen interest in taekwondo. I took all the classes at Maher and earned a black belt. In school, I completed a Bachelor of Arts in Business Communication.

For many years I dreamed of joining the Maharashtra Police Service. Maher helped me take admission at Dream Academy in Hadapsar for professional guidance and practice related to Police Service. After that, I was selected for the Maharashtra Police Department. I then went through police training and completed it. Now I am a policeman in Pune City.

Meanwhile, when we arrived at Maher, my mother began working as a housemother in one of Maher's children's homes. During this time, she studied and completed her education and then took Maher's para-social worker training. She is now social-worker-in-charge at two Maher homes. Everyone says she is a wonderful social worker.

Now my mother, my younger sister and I live together outside Maher. Between my salary and my mother's salary from Maher it is enough to support the family. We are independent now. It feels very satisfying!

Stories from Maher

From Maher to Homeless Soccer
World Cup Games in Chile:
Mahika's Story
Mahika wrote her story for Maher.

I lived in various NGOs, beginning when I was sixteen months old. I was the only child of my parents. When I was a baby, my father left and married another woman. My mother was not in a position to look after me because of poverty and illness. Sometimes I would be in an NGO for care, then my mother would come bring me home again when she was able. My mother was literate and she was determined that I too would be educated. When I was old enough for school I went to another NGO for education. My mother and I were very close, even though I was in a boarding school.

When my mother fell very ill and she knew that she was not going to live long, she put me into another NGO for full shelter and education. I was in the fourth standard when my mother died. I went into shock and fell very ill. I became mentally very disturbed and could not complete my fourth standard. It took me some years to recover and get back to normal. Meanwhile, I was sent to several different NGOs. I was a very troublesome child because I was so upset and sad to be an orphan.

Finally, I came to Pune and was sent by the Child Welfare Committee to Maher. At this point I was in the

RISING TO NEW LIFE

tenth standard. My situation felt very hopeless.

After this, my life totally changed under the love, care and guidance of Sister Lucy Kurien, the Founder of Maher. There was no more looking back. I became very happy. I continued my education and became a serious soccer player. I played soccer in many tournaments.

While studying in the twelfth standard, I got the opportunity to represent Maher on India's Slum Soccer Women's Team. In 2014, my team earned a trip to the International Homeless Soccer World Cup[23] in Santiago Chile.

Another girl, Jahnavi, came to Maher the same year as I did and was also an orphan (though she came with her brother and sister). We both excelled in soccer and played on the same teams. We both earned positions on India's Slum Soccer Team. We journeyed together to Chile to play in the Homeless Soccer World Cup, which made the whole experience even better!

I am so very grateful to Sister Lucy for giving me this opportunity! I look forward to a bright future. I have no other family; Maher is my only hope and home.

---

[23] The Mission of International Homeless Soccer, per their website, is to use football to support and inspire young people who are homeless to change their own lives; and to change perceptions and attitudes towards people who are experiencing homelessness.

Stories from Maher

From Desperately Poor Tribal Village to Leadership:
Yadavi's Story

Note: Yadavi's family comes from a tribal village where Maher began outreach work in 1999.[24] The poverty was extreme: they lived in mud huts, survived on leftover food scraps from the fields where they labored, no one attended school, no one was literate. Yadavi was about five years old then. Slowly Maher brought education to the children (and adults). Later, Maher built a small residential home there for children to receive a full education, food, security, and all needs taken care of. Yadavi was in that first class. This story was written by Yadavi, with additional information from Sister Lucy.

I was a small girl. We were very poor and faced extreme poverty. In the year 2005, I came to the new Maher Home in my village. I was in eighth standard. I was determined and happy that I was able to complete my tenth standard.

After I completed my tenth standard, I came to the Aboli Home at Maher Vadhu Center. I had the opportunity to work in the Production Center and learned to make a lot of products. I was able to adjust

---

[24] *For more about Maher's development work in villages and tribal areas, see forthcoming book.*

RISING TO NEW LIFE

to the culture and wanted to study further. I completed my eleventh and twelfth standard and then went to a college in Koregaon, walking distance from Vadhu Budruk. Later I did my ANM nursing training at Tarachand Hospital for one and a half years. I was very happy that I was able to complete my course and grateful for the whole-hearted support from Maher.

Sister Lucy added: after Yadavi completed twelfth standard, her parents were pushing to get her married. I convinced them to wait and let Yadavi get training in a skill for a better job. This way Yadavi was able to attend nursing training. Then she got a job at the local hospital. After this I told the family that now they can arrange a marriage for Yadavi.

Yadavi continued: in 2015 I was pleased to be married to Girish. I went to live with him and was a housewife. I was very interested to become a police officer, so I completed the application form for the Police Patil exam. I passed the examination and became a Police Patil, "chief person" for her village.

Sister Lucy clarified: now she is a "vigilant" for her village. She is a leader now in her village, one who looks after the village, a sort of government liaison. If anyone in the village has a problem they go to her. One example is for help to appeal to the government for

Stories from Maher

aid: Yadavi needs to write a recommendation letter to the government on their behalf. She organizes many things in her village like that. It's a big post!

Yadavi continued: I received a lot of support from the villagers and did a lot of good work. Everyone cooperated with me. I now have two children: a four-and-a-half-year-old son and a one-month-old baby girl. What I am today and all that I could accomplish was only because of the love, encouragement and support I received from Maher.

From Sr Lucy: Yadavi was the first woman, even the first person, from her village to get this level of education. She was so shy and sweet when I first met her, and each year I would see more confidence and poise in her. Wow!

Final note: this author met Yadavi in 2010 shortly after she came to live in Aboli house. She was very shy. She had only a few words of English and I had only a few in Marathi, but we connected with lots of smiles. Yadavi was always eager to help people. While I was in Pune during the day, she would take my washing off the clothesline and iron it dry for me. (It was the rainy season—nothing really ever dried!) I would find my clothes dry and ironed in my room. She also ironed my sari for me—that is the most fascinating process. Saris are very long rectangles of cloth 45 inches wide and 15-30 feet long (4.5-9 meters long). There are no ironing boards, she ironed it the traditional Indian way. There is an intricate process of folding, ironing the top bit, refolding and ironing, refolding and ironing, etc. that boggles my mind! How do they know they got it all? But she did! It is extra special to see her now with a husband, a family and taking a leadership role in her village!

Even Sister Lucy Can't Save Everyone: Yashoda's Story
Narrated by Sister Lucy.

Yashoda Sagar was brought to Maher by a children's home in Mumbai. She was wearing boys clothing. Staff guessed her age to be about fifteen years old. No one knows how many years she had been surviving alone on the streets.

Yashoda said she used the name Sagar, a boy's name, because she was living on the streets. When she was about fifteen years old, the police caught her and took her to a children's home in Mumbai. They thought she was a boy because she was dressed in male clothes and therefore placed her in the boy's home. The boys in the home soon found out she was a girl and reported it to the Superintendent. The police

Stories from Maher

came to the home and beat her up. They thought that she was bluffing them; they did not understand why she chose to look like a boy.

After three days she was shifted to the girl's home. Yashoda said she found it very difficult to be a girl. For years she had dressed like a boy. Even now she said she finds it very difficult to be a girl. The children's home had troubles with her and thought she would be better off at Maher. They brought her here.

Slowly Yashoda told me more of her history. She said that she did not know her real name. She had a name tattooed on her arm: "Yashoda." So she thought that was her name and that is why she gave her name as Yashoda. Yashoda said that she did not know how she ended up on the streets in Mumbai. She said she learned to speak Hindi and Marathi on the streets.

I asked her how she managed to have clothes to wear.

Yashoda explained there were many people who left old clothes at bus stops and railway stations.

I asked her how she managed to live in the cold and in the rain.

Yashoda said sometimes she slept at the railway station, sometimes at a bus stop, and sometimes on the veranda of a shop. She said she must have slept in a thousand different places.

I asked her why she changed her place of sleep.

Yashoda said the police and other people used to

RISING TO NEW LIFE

keep an eye on her and often hurt her, so she kept moving.

Then I asked why she liked boy's clothes.

Yashoda said that it was not that she liked the boy's clothes; it was because she learned it was much safer to dress and look like a boy. As a girl she was raped often. She said she remembered being about four years old when men first tried to rape her.

Once she told her story, we helped her learn to become a girl again. She grew out her hair, wore women's clothing, and had counseling, all to help her learn to be a girl and to adjust to life at Maher. Yashoda said she wanted to study and "to be someone."

Yashoda became happy here and wanted to go to school. Maher gave her new girl's school uniforms, a bookbag and all she needed for school. At first, the school said they would not take her because it was mid-term. Also, she had no papers from her previous school. Finally, the school agreed to let her just sit in class, though not officially a student. She was happily reading and studying so I suspected she must have had some education already.

Then one day Yashoda ran away from the school. She must have hidden clothes in her school bag. She was used to being free. This is a challenge with all the children who have lived on the streets.

We searched for her and filed a missing person case with the police. After six months, the police phoned

106

Stories from Maher

from Madhya Pradesh[25]. They found her and because she had asked to be returned to Maher, the police brought her back here to Pune. Because she had been gone for so long, she had to first go to the Child Welfare Committee and then she could come back to Maher.

Yashoda said she wanted to go back to school, but the school was not ready to take her back because she ran away. We begged the principal. Finally, he agreed. Then she again left school; she said she didn't want school anymore. Next, we put her in the Production Center, stitching cloth bags and cards.

After about six months, again she ran away from Maher. Again, we searched and filed a missing person case. We didn't have a birth certificate or any official paper with her birthday, but we did not think she was eighteen yet.

Often she phoned us, sometimes to me, sometimes to different staff. We all said please come back, we love you. But she wouldn't tell anyone where she was. On December twenty-fourth she phoned me, but Maher was holding the annual holiday program. With all the loudspeaker noise, I didn't hear my phone ringing. As soon as I saw the missed call, I tried to call back.

Sadly, Yashoda was already dead and could not answer. It turned out that she was with a boy and got pregnant. We learned that several boys raped her,

---

[25] Madhya Pradesh is a state north of Pune in central India

murdered her, and hung her. The report said she was already dead when they hung her from a soccer goal post. This happened several states away, and the story was in all the newspapers.

After she ran away, this time we went through her things. We were very surprised to find a map of where she was from, her address, even how to get to her house in her village. We gave this to the police. They went to her family. Then we learned she was already eighteen years old. But by this time, she had already died. Why did she never even admit to having a family? What had gone wrong there that led her to live on the streets? We will never know.

I was so torn up from Yashoda's violent death, even though there was likely nothing I could have done from so far away to save her life. It is so sad. A child on the streets since she was small ... all those years of having no shelter, no safety, no love. Her story still hurts my heart.

Abandoned: A Beautiful Boy

This story is based on this author's meeting this young man, plus what I learned from Sister Lucy.

One day while visiting Maher's Men's Home for old, mentally disturbed, disabled, and abandoned men, I was captivated by the most beautiful pale sea green eyes and big broad smile. The young man was wearing

Stories from Maher

a black knit cap and sitting in a circle of men who were tossing a ball back and forth among themselves. I wondered about his story and why he was there. Sister Lucy's driver, Balu, was my guide that day and he called the boy over to us. I noticed the boy's gait was off: he pulled his left leg along.

Balu asked the boy to remove his hat. The whole right side of his head looked partly caved in, like that side of his brain was missing. I could see his left hand and lower arm hung limp and slightly curled, clearly not very usable. But he continued with his beautiful smile, gazing at us with bright eyes. He could speak with Balu, but it was limited. He said he was not in pain. Indeed, he appeared quite happy. He continued smiling all the while we visited with him.

Later this author asked Sister Lucy for more of his story. She continued:

We picked him up from under a bridge several years ago. Someone had found him there and called us. We sent a social worker right away to pick him up.

He had a very big lump on the side of his head. At this time he could not speak. He could not tell us anything about who he was, where he came from, what was the lump on his head. Nothing.

At first, we thought perhaps he had been born that way. We took him to the hospital for a full examination. The doctors did an MRI and they found a brain tumor.

It was very large and very serious.

The doctors managed to operate and remove most of it, maybe even all of it. They explained that the tumor was so large and had been there so long that his whole nervous system was affected. His left hand was affected. His left leg. His speech. His eye on the left; he could not see properly.

He was in a coma for three months in the hospital, then in the ICU. He had chemotherapy and radiation; it was a long time. We had to keep two staff people in the hospital to care for him during all this time.[26] We thought maybe he would never recover. The doctors did a really good job. If this had been done earlier, it would have been easier, but still they believe the tumor is gone now.

It took almost one year for him to be able to take care of his own hygiene (toilet, bath, etc.) and to walk a little. He is improving. He is now able to express his needs, walk around, take care of himself. Slowly, miraculously, he has regained his eyesight. And he has regained some ability to speak. He doesn't have headaches anymore. He had physical therapy from the hospital, but that is finished.

My guess is that he might have been slightly mentally retarded. Plus, he had the tumor, which could have frightened his family. We really couldn't learn

---

[26] In India, families provide the nursing care unless they are quite wealthy and can hire this.

Stories from Maher

much from him about his past, his background, or how he ended up under the bridge. He said simply that when he was small someone put him there. Maybe because of the combination of the lump on his head and the mental weakness, the family felt they could not care for him, and they abandoned him. He must have already been living there for a few years when we found him.

Now he has been with us for almost three years. He is very happy.

Chapter 5: Babies at Maher (Born Here or Found with Their Mother)

Raised by Maher Staff from Birth: Zuri's Story

Sister Lucy told this story. This author believes Lucy falls in love with every baby at Maher!

We found Zuri's mother eight months pregnant and living on the street. She was clearly mentally disturbed when we first brought her to Maher. We believe this girl was raped so no one knows who Zuri's father was. We got her medical attention and took care of her before and after the delivery.

It was a challenge to look after her: she would jump over the gate and run away, even when she was still pregnant. One time she did this, she fractured her leg. She was very agitated.

We got her through the delivery. Thankfully, it was a normal delivery. The mother, however, was still too agitated to care for her child. She seemed disconnected from her baby. All the time she would run. We did not know where she was wanting to run to or why. Finally, one day she managed to escape from

Stories from Maher

Maher. We could not find her.

To keep any child born here, we have to apply to the government. We must prove that the baby has no family who can provide adequate care. We did finally learn something of the mother's background; we found her father and brother. Her father was "IQ-less": all he could do was say his name. His wife was long gone. Maher was allowed to keep Zuri because it was clear the mother's family was unable to care for the baby. We also learned that there was another girl, about nineteen or twenty years old, sister to Zuri's mother, who was also mentally not fully ok. Because the living conditions were so bad, we brought this sister back to Maher. But she went back to the father; without her there was no one to cook the food for him.

We continue to care for the child and will raise her to adulthood with all the benefits of Maher. Zuri is now in the first standard and loved by all.

Child Born of a Child: Anika and Binita
Narrated by Sister Lucy.

Anika was thirteen when she delivered Binita, a baby girl. Anika, a child herself, was deaf and dumb. Her mother was an alcoholic. They lived under a tree. When Anika became pregnant her alcoholic mother was not even aware her daughter was pregnant.

Someone came and told us that there was a baby

living under a tree. They said that the baby was in danger, and the child-mother also needed care. These people were from a well-known organization. They brought the baby and her mother to Maher. The baby was likely no more than a few days old.

When I first held baby Binita she fit in my hand—she weighed only 800 grams, or just under 2 pounds. Her hands were so thin, her whole hand was as big as my thumb. As far as we can guess, when Anika delivered, it must have been under that tree. Someone must have helped her because the umbilical cord was cut. But then they must have left them.

Straight away we took both Anika and Binita to the hospital because they were both malnourished and sickly. I did not think Binita would even survive, but she did. We were able to bring both mother and baby back to Maher. We settled them in Aboli Home with all the college-going girls and staff to help with their care.

Anika was herself a child, barely thirteen, so of course she had no idea how to care for a baby. She was also deaf and dumb, so she had no idea what even happened to her, or what was going on in the ordinary world. No one had ever cared for her. It was very difficult to communicate with her at all.

At Maher, Anika would run to play on the swings, leaving her baby. The baby sometimes got sick, because Anika didn't know how to care for her properly. We too had trouble feeding the baby—we

Stories from Maher

could not make Anika to understand how or when to breast feed her baby.

Sister Sister Meena or I would get up in the night to hold baby Binita on her mother's breast to feed the baby. We also gave the baby extra milk. That is how we kept the baby and mother alive.

When the baby was almost two, we stopped the breast feeding and we sent the mother Anika to a special school for the deaf and dumb. This year she will complete her tenth standard, after only about three or four years of school!

Binita remained in Aboli House where the older college-going girls helped to care for her. During the day many staff work there as well. Binita was the darling girl and was showered with love and attention.

When Binita was nearing school age, she went to live in one of the Pune houses so she could begin school at one of the English-medium schools there. Binita is now in first standard.

Little Binita has adjusted well from being nearly the only small child in a house of adults and everyone's darling, to life in a large houseful of children of varying ages. Now she is the darling of the bigger children and housemothers in Pune. For holidays she comes "home" to Vadhu; to Binita, Vadhu is her home and the Pune house is her boarding school home.

Sometimes It's Tricky to Do the Best for

RISING TO NEW LIFE

the Child and Still Follow The Rules:
Chaya's Story

Children's backgrounds can be complicated, Maher must tread carefully to keep these children. Sister Lucy told this story as one example.

Chaya's mother brought her to Maher when she was not even one year old. The mother had cancer and she said the father is not at all interested in the baby. We wondered about this; government rules are very strict which children we can take in. Also, they came from Mumbai, and we are not supposed to keep a baby from another district. If we break the rules, this can endanger our license and therefore all the children. We wanted also to help the mother with her cancer treatments. For now, we kept the baby girl with us. The mother remained in Mumbai and took treatment for her cancer.

Maher staff made the trip to Mumbai, to see what we could learn. We found the family and the husband; it was a mess.

When the mother was just out of a round of cancer treatment, and I could talk to her again, I asked her for the truth: what really has happened?

She said Chaya was her second "husband's" child. Her real husband and two children were living in another place. She fell in love with another man and left to live with him. They could not marry of course

Stories from Maher

because she was already married. After some time, Chaya was born.

But then this man started disliking her. Then she got cancer, and the man would not look at her at all. Neither her first husband, nor her two sons who were older, would take her in, because she made a mistake. They would not even come and see her. This is how it was.

Meanwhile, Chaya continued to live at Maher, but the mother stopped coming to see her. We didn't know if she was still alive. We went to the hospital where she was getting the cancer treatment. They told us she had not come back for her next chemotherapy treatment. They also did not know where she was.

We called to the first, legal, husband and asked where she was. He told us she died. We asked where did she die—which hospital? He was not able to say. So we went to the house of Chaya's father but he had moved. We could not find him. Given all this, we could not get a death certificate. Neither of the men wanted Chaya, so we were able to keep her with us.

Chaya is such a sweet child. She is growing up very nicely. We enrolled her in a very good kindergarten school which will prepare her for English-medium school. She will do well, we hope.

RISING TO NEW LIFE

Raising a Toddler When His Mother Is Unable: Ganga's Story

Sister Lucy's "mother's heart" is so big—her heart hears all the cries. She told this story.

Ganga's mother was found on the streets, totally mentally disturbed. We don't know her story, nor how she and her son came to be on the streets. He was already over one year old when we found them. It was clear right away that she was not ok mentally. We noticed that she didn't seem to understand he was a baby and growing. She didn't know how to hold him: she held him around his ribs, legs dangling, carrying him like a sack of potatoes. He had never been allowed to crawl, let alone walk.

Right away we got them both medical examinations and a psychological assessment for her. She is now receiving care at Maher's Vatsalydham Home. She is incapable of the care Ganga needs. So he is at Aboli where there are always lots of people, both staff and the college-going girls.

He cries at night. He just wants to be held. He presses his head to my shoulder. He only needs a few minutes. Then he's ok.

Staff told me to just let him cry and he will go back to sleep. They know this disturbs my sleep and they worry about me. But I hear him cry and I am the one who gets up, even though others are closer. To hear him cry, it turns my stomach.

For now, he needs to learn that he can cry and someone will soothe him. He didn't have this for the first year and a half of his life. So he will get what he needs now, and then as he grows, as he becomes more secure, he won't need this.

When Ganga first arrived, though he was about one and a half years old, he did not know how to walk because of the way his mother had carried him. His legs didn't even work right. Even now his legs are wobbly and he is bow-legged, but he is learning to walk. I watch him determinedly walk up steps and then back down, back and forth, sort of stomping his tiny feet to feel the earth. His legs are strengthening daily. He is so determined to walk!

Ganga is also very clever. He came over to us just now. He could tell we were busy, so he went away again. He will come back later, when we pause. For now, he found someone else to interact with. He reads people.

Author observations:

This author met sweet little Ganga on my most recent visit to Maher. When I met him, he was nearly two years old and had been at Maher for just a few months. He was very slender and petite. His big brown eyes closely watched everyone and everything. He was quiet, yet oh so curious!

Rising to New Life

Another example of how curious and clever he is, was watching him learn to dip a cup in the water urn. In India it is common to have a big steel urn with a relatively narrow opening sitting on a table with a single communal cup. To get a drink you dip the cup in, using two fingers, and then pour water into your mouth without touching your lips to the cup. Ganga had watched for several days how the adults dipped into the water urn with the one cup provided and took a drink, without touching the rim of the cup. Finally, he tried to do it just like the big people did. This urn sat on a low table about as tall as he is, so this took quite a bit of dexterity to accomplish, and he only dribbled a little bit!

Mostly Ganga is happy and he is one of the joys of Maher. He steals the heart of everyone with his love and laughter. His baby language is so soothing to listen to. He is loved and cared for by all. When he is older, he too will be shifted to Pune to attend an English-medium school.

Sister Lucy with a group of the earliest children.

Housemothers and children outside Mogra House, part of Vadhu Center. This is a typical size "family" for one Home with the smaller children. (Older children might be closer to twenty-five children.)

Prem Sagar Home in Pune. All Homes must be gated for security of the children, per Indian law.

From right: Hira, Darcy handing out candy to each child. A group gathered (about 400?) for a program. The children sit together as a Home unit, then at the end, queue up as a group to get their treat! Very polite and orderly!

Suprabha, a senior social worker, with a young girl resident.

Maya, social worker for Apti Village, near Vadhu, with a group of school children. Her responsibilities include the Maher Home there, plus the whole village and surrounding area.

Gaus, Mangesh and other boys rehearsing a Bollywood dance they choreographed to "Jai Ho!" (from film Slum Dog Millionaire)

Two of the Maher young people performing a Katuk dance.

Taekwondo is for both the girls and boys! Here the girls are performing, showing their kicks to a target stick (at left edge of photo). This sport is loved by many of the children and is a great outlet for high energy, as well as helpful for processing difficult emotions.

Two boys doing a taekwondo demonstration.

When Maher picks up people they find on the streets, often the first thing is to offer food and water. Later, once trust is built, they will get a bath, clean clothes, and then medical attention.

Sometimes the people are unclothed, or only partially clothed. Often they are fearful, confused, starving, even ill, depending on how long they have been on the streets.

Sukh Sandhya is Maher's project for homeless elderly women. There are multiple Sukh Sandhya Homes spread across Maher's sites. They all adore Sister Lucy-and she loves all of them!

Maher also picks up men abandoned and homeless. Karunalaya is Maher's project for mentally disturbed and homeless men. There are multiple such homes spread across Maher's sites.

Women residents stitching greeting cards in Production at Vadhu. This is a soothing social activity for the women, plus they earn income from each piece they stitch. The colorful stitched cards are lovely and popular with friends of Maher who purchase Production items.

Also in Production, women learn machine stitching, from making the simple purses and pouches, to tailoring clothing. Again they earn income from each piece, plus learn a highly marketable skill.

When women residents give birth, Maher holds naming ceremonies and gives gifts to the new mother and child.

Maher frequently holds large gatherings to celebrate national and religious holidays, such as Eid, Christmas, International Women's Day, Divali, Gandhi's birthday, and many more. Fun for all!

When volunteers come and go, Maher plans welcome and farewell programs, as with my arrival for 2020 visit. Meditation, felicitation, singing, and snacks are usually part of the programs! Adults from left: Hira, two Maher residents, Sister Lucy, Darcy, Mangesh. You can see one large group of children behind us, but there are two more even larger groups to the right and across from us!

Interfaith wedding of Gaus and Padmini (see Chapter 7). Sister Lucy and the couple are holding the marriage certificate, surrounded by priests of different religions who were part of the ceremonies: Buddhist monk, Maulana (Muslim Priest), Catholic Priest, and Hindu Pujari.

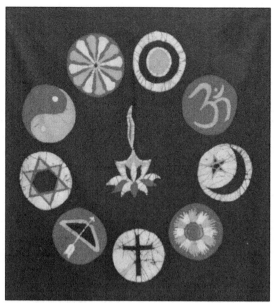

Maher's banner of religions representing the most common religions found in India.

Mangesh and Maher young people at an Interfaith program. Maher works hard to foster tolerance of all religions well beyond Maher's doors.

Housewarming and blessing for two Maher boys, Yogesh and his brother Nandu, as they move into their new home, built adjacent to Vadhu. From left to right, unmasked, Nandu, Yogesh, Sister Lucy.(See Chapter 7)

Sister Lucy and the author, Darcy.

Sister Lucy with her parents.

Chapter 6: Families

Tragedy Strikes:
the Story of Deepa and Her Son, Raj

Sister Lucy told most of this story, with a few additions from Raj himself.

Deepa arrived at Maher in 2003 with her nine-year-old son Raj. Deepa seemed totally mad and Raj was confused. They were both so dirty that no one wanted to touch them. The boy had been begging on the streets to fill his belly and to keep his mother alive. We fed them, cleaned them up, and took them for medical and psychological evaluation. Deepa was so traumatized that she could not tell us anything at first. She began medication and treatment.

We did not know how they came to Pune or to Maher. Raj told us what he recalled, and later, when Deepa had healed enough to recall what happened, she began to tell us what she remembered. Slowly we pieced together their story.

Deepa and her husband had two boys: Raj, age four, and a baby. Deepa's husband had gone to Mumbai in search of a job. Her husband did not return home for

Stories from Maher

some time. She was desperate and traveled from her village to Mumbai in search of her husband.

Alternatively, Raj said he thought he recalled that his parents had some fight and his father left. His mother did not have work, so she could not feed the children or pay the rent. They were forced to leave their home and they were living on the streets and in railway stations. The family begged for food and so started their begging life. He said his mother was very determined to work so they left their village to go to the city to find work. This was why they travelled to Mumbai.

Whatever actually happened to bring them to Mumbai, both agree as to the tragedy that occurred.

In Mumbai the local trains were electric. Therefore they were much faster and quieter, compared to the village trains with which Deepa was familiar. The stops at each station were very brief, unlike the rural trains. She got onto a train with her younger son and her bag. She settled them on the train. Then she went back down to pick up four-year-old Raj. As she was trying to re-board with Raj, the train left. She fell down from the train along with Raj. No one stopped the train and it was gone. She lay there unconscious, bleeding from the head; people took her and Raj to the hospital. When she awoke she asked after her two boys. Only Raj was there. She was frantic. Wailing. She did not remember where the train had been heading. In

RISING TO NEW LIFE

Mumbai the electric local trains go through every five minutes. No one knew where the baby boy ended up and he was never found. She got depressed and finally became mad.

It was five years before they ended up at Maher. Little Raj, from age four up to age nine, somehow took care of his mother and himself all this time! He learned to beg and steal food for her and take her places to sleep. Deepa was afraid to let him out of her sight, in case she lost him, too. People would tell him that his mother was mad, and he should take her to the hospital. He didn't understand what "mad" meant. By this time, this was all he knew; this was just how his mother was.

Through all this time, from age four to age nine, the little boy had taken care of his mother as best he could. Somehow, he got them from Mumbai to Pune. Raj later recalled how they came to Maher. He told us that when they were on the streets, one day a journalist saw them. Deepa was not in any condition to talk with him and so he asked Raj about their story. The man decided to put their story in the newspaper. After that story many helping hands came forward to offer support. And this is how they ultimately found Maher.

Soon after they arrived, our social workers enrolled Raj in the local school. At age nine he had never attended school, so he had to start in first standard. He was very bright and very determined. He did two

Stories from Maher

months in first standard, then the exam. Then two months in second standard, then the exam. Same for third standard. Then he was in fourth standard for the completion of school year and exam. In one year he had caught up with the other children his age!

While Raj was in school, Deepa too lived at our main center at Vadhu. (This was before we had a project focused on the needs of mentally disturbed women.) At first, she was very disturbed. When she heard a truck passing, she would think it was a train. She would race toward the road shouting her baby son's name. "Ammen! Ammen!" She would chase the truck down the street calling out his name. Staff raced after her, afraid that when she stopped running, she would not know how to get back to Maher. If we tried to grab her, she fought—and she was strong! She even punched me once! Staff learned to follow in the car. The first time we picked her up in the car, she smashed the window trying to get back out, thinking she could get to her baby. So we learned we needed to approach quietly from behind and bind her wrists to get her into the car safely. It was heartbreaking to witness.

We made many inquiries trying to find what happened to this baby, but we never found him. Slowly Deepa began to accept that she would likely never find her lost baby son. She regained enough of her mind for simple work. She would stand at the gate of Maher on the side of the street where the children's homes are, across from the office. She helped the small children cross. She was there every day. She smiled to staff, guests, and residents, whoever walked back and forth.

A few years ago, we finally located Deepa's husband, Raj's father. He came to Pune to see them. In the intervening time, about fourteen or more years, he had remarried, not knowing where his family had disappeared to. Deepa said, "It has been so long. He has a new life; let him be." She said she was ok at Maher. This was very reasonable. I felt this was a sign she had truly stabilized.

Meanwhile, Raj participated in all Maher had to offer: sports, dance, education and travel. He was part of the Maher dance group who traveled to the U.K. in 2007. He competed nationally in dance and soccer. Raj attended college and university. While in college, he was selected to attend the Global Leadership Forum, run by UWC (United World Colleges), in the U.S. At University he earned a Bachelor of Arts degree. Now he has a good job at an insurance company in Pune. He married a Maher girl who works as a nurse. They live well and independently. They still visit Maher on special occasions. Recently he brought Deepa home to live with him. He wrote that he is grateful to be able to give her the life she should have had. He says his dream is to take Maher and Maher's values forward and to give back to society.

A Family Comes to Maher:

Stories from Maher

the Stories of Varsha, Vikram, and Their Mother

Sister Lucy told the family story, then Varsha's; Vikram wrote his own story for this book.

The family lived in Talegaon Dhamdare [a village in Pune District]. Two children, first a boy and then a girl, were born here. The father was addicted to alcohol. His health declined due to alcohol addiction and in 2002 he passed away.

After the death of her husband, their mother worked as a house maid. But it was very difficult for her to take care of both children, plus she did not have any education. Because she was a widow, no one wanted her; none of the relatives were supportive. It was a very difficult time for the family.

Like any mother, she wanted her children to have a better life. Someone told her about Maher, so she came here with her daughter Varsha. Varsha was small, about nine years old. We took them in. The mother began working as a housemother at Maher.

One day she told me she wanted to go out. I asked her why? Where are you going? She didn't want to tell me, but I persisted. Finally, she admitted she had a son, but he was in another institution. She had managed to place the boy, Vikram, in a school nearby. She said she was afraid to come to Maher with two children: she worried Maher would turn her and her children away. She thought, then who would look after me and my two children? So she placed her son, who is the older child, in one institution and came to Maher with her small daughter.

Of course, we wanted to help the family be together, so I sent a social worker with her to collect Vikram and bring him back to Maher. Both children attended school and all the other activities for children here.

Mama continued working as a housemother and she learned well. But she got more and more depressed. She wanted to remarry but her culture didn't allow widows to remarry. She longed for a home, for a companion. We could see this, but we could also see she dared not take the steps. I encouraged her to try it. The woman was afraid though. She worried her in-laws would cut them off. Her children would be unable to marry due to the shame. So she remained here without getting married.

She got more and more depressed, nearly mad. Her veins in her legs started bleeding and bursting and we could not heal it. One would break, she would go to the hospital, bleeding and bleeding. We would heal that one, then the next would break. Again and again like this. Finally, she died of this. She got too weak, which worsened the depression.

When she was dying, she begged me to keep and raise her children, to not give them away to anyone. Of course both children remained at Maher. Both the children completed schooling and earned Masters' in

Stories from Maher

Social Work. Both are now working at Maher as social workers.

Varsha's story as told by Sister Lucy:
Varsha works at Vatsalydam with the mentally disturbed women. She is a wonderful social worker, but I wanted her to also get married and have her own family. In Varsha's caste the women get married by twenty-three. She was twenty-eight and I was getting very worried that she would not be able to get married. I would find good men whom I wanted to introduce, but she kept refusing to marry. She kept delaying and delaying. She was afraid to leave Maher. She knew if she married, she would have to live outside Maher. This was why she kept refusing to marry.

I longed for Varsha to experience living in a family, and the joy of having a family, as I had known. This is why I told Varsha she needed to marry. Oh, Varsha fought with me about this! I told her: If you don't like the men I am choosing, then you go find one you like! Enough is enough! I kept pushing. Finally, she found a man, a really wonderful man. He is of the same caste and has a good job as an accountant in a company. They got married. Varsha now lives outside Maher with her husband and his family, but still works at Maher. She is so happy!

On their first anniversary Varsha invited me to have dinner there with her friends and relatives. She said to me: you educated me, you gave me everything, and I am grateful for all you have done. But even more because you gave me a family. I am so grateful to you! She cried, hugging me, her head on my shoulder. I was so happy to see how happy Varsha was. Varsha told me that she was so afraid she would not get a good family, that she would be miserable like her mother was, and end up with her children in an institution. She said she was so afraid of all that; that is why she wouldn't marry.

Varsha said that God has chosen the best for her, she can see this now. She said she thought I didn't love her and that's why I wanted her to marry and go away. She thought I wanted to get rid of her. She said she didn't understand that I was wishing for the best life for her. She was doubting me. She told me she talked to others on the staff about this, and they all assured her that I was doing this because I loved her. She said it was so hard for her to believe—if I loved her how could I get rid of her? She wanted me to know that now she understood.

I was so surprised; I didn't know that Varsha had been thinking this way. So I just listened. I only did this because I loved her. It was so wonderful to hear all she was saying and to know she understands now and is so happy!

Vikram's story, in his own words:

Stories from Maher

After we came to Maher our life got changed. We received lots of love and care from Sister Lucy and our Maher family. After I finished my tenth standard education, Didi gave me permission for further education. I completed college and University.

In Maher I got opportunities to learn many things. Didi provided me the opportunity to participate in sports, competitions, and various camps. The biggest opportunity was for me to attend an International Peace Camp in the U.S. I was there for one month and learned so many things in that period. I am so grateful to Maher and Sister Lucy to provide me this wonderful opportunity.

After that, based on my interest in social work, Maher helped me to gain admission for a Master's in Social Work degree. Now I am working at Maher as a social worker, helping Sister Lucy to fulfill her dream and helping the needy. I am based in the Vadhu Center, working with the children. I am so grateful to all the Maher family and dearest Sister Lucy for their love and care for my family. They have stood beside me in every stage of my life. Whatever things I achieved in my life, that is because of Maher and Didi. I am so grateful.

RISING TO NEW LIFE

Helping One Person Lifts the Generations to Come: Eshana and Her Family

This story begins in the early days of Maher and continues through the present day and includes a third generation. This family's path offers a good overview of Maher's work over a twenty-three-year timespan, showing the long-term relationships, the back and forth, in and out of Maher, that can happen with families, and the growth over time in what Maher can offer to people. This family would have been destitute had their paths not crossed with Hira, Sister Lucy and Maher in 1999. Instead, all three generations are thriving.

Before coming to work at Maher, Hirabegum Mullah was doing some advanced social worker training in aftercare and psychosocial care at Sassoon Hospital Psychiatric Department when her teacher connected her to Eshana, a woman who had come seeking help. Hira soon completed her studies and went to work at Maher as its first social worker in 1999; she essentially brought Eshana with her. Below is Hira's account of Eshana and her family.

Eshana, from a village about 240 kilometers from Pune, had come here for medical treatment. After she shared her troubles, Sassoon Hospital Psychiatric Department referred her to Maher to meet Sister Lucy. She had four children: two girls and two boys. At this

Stories from Maher

time, she only had her elder daughter and youngest son with her while the other two were still at home with their father. She was mentally disturbed due to trauma and had barely any idea what she was saying or doing. Seeing the plight of the mother and children, Sister Lucy admitted them into Maher.

At Maher, once the burden of caring for the children was taken away, Eshana's mental condition started to improve. As Eshana began to recover, she was able to tell us her story.

Eshana told us that she was married at the age of eleven to a man who was a slow learner. She had her first baby at the age of thirteen. She conducted her own delivery; she had no one to help her nor any money to travel to a hospital. This first baby died. The second baby was born when Eshana was fifteen, again at home. She cut the umbilical cord with the kitchen knife. This baby survived as did the next three. The sixth baby died. The four surviving children all eventually came to Maher. The husband remained at home during all of this.

She and the children did not stay long this first time. When Eshana was mentally stable again, she and her children left Maher. She returned to her village to care for her husband and all four children. She got Prisha, the eldest girl who was fifteen years old, married. This marriage did not go well.

In 2001 Eshana returned to Maher, this time

bringing all three children still at home. Soon after, she rescued Prisha from the bad marriage and brought her to Maher as well. The children's ages at this point ranged from about ten to sixteen and none had attended school. Now we could see to an education for all the children. They all eventually completed tenth standard and went on to further training, all under our care.

We also helped Eshana earn her tenth standard certification and then train as a kindergarten teacher. Eshana left Maher again to return to her village to care for her husband and work at a kindergarten. She has since received awards for her work at this kindergarten.

Eshana's children's stories: the boys' stories:
At the time the family came to us, Maher did not have a separate home for boys. Boys over age twelve must be housed separately by law in Maharashtra state so we could not keep the boys with us after age twelve. Fortunately, Agnel Ashram opened a home for boys in Pune. The older boy, Achal, and soon his younger brother, Tharshan, were sent there until completion of tenth standard.

After tenth standard, we took Achal, and later Tharshan, to Mumbai to Washi village and enrolled them in technical college per their wishes. They completed their studies and earned technical degrees.

Stories from Maher

Achal is married now and working in Mumbai; he has two children. Tharshan was hired by a company and sent to the U.S. for further training. He later returned to India and worked in a different state. He married. His wife is a lawyer. They have one girl child. His wife is pregnant again now, so she is not working. He later got a new job in Mumbai working on the oil rigs for one to two months at a time.

Prisha's story:

When Prisha was about fifteen years old, her mother got her married to her husband's sister's son. She didn't know how to cook the food or other work expected of a wife, so the husband's family gave her lots of trouble. They even tried to kill her by adding poison to her food, or sometimes crushed glass. When her mother came to know, she brought Prisha back to Maher where she and the other children were living.

Prisha wanted to study but she had essentially no prior schooling. As she was sixteen years old, we enrolled her in a residential adult literacy school in Pune. In three years, she completed her eighth, ninth and tenth standard exams. Anand, the other Maher social worker, and I visited her every month. We brought her snacks, paid for her books and school fees, and made sure she was doing well. After that Prisha wanted to do nursing training. So, we found a good residential nursing program and enrolled her.

She got scared with all the blood and could not complete the course, so she returned to Maher.

Prisha decided she wanted to learn tailoring. She began working in Maher's Production Center, where we taught her tailoring and other skills. She learned these well. She then said she wanted to go back home and live with her mother and father since they were alone now. She would do tailoring work in the village to earn money. We gave her a sewing machine and sent her home.

Several years later Maher opened the Miraj Center, several hours from Pune. Miraj is near the village where Prisha's parents live. When Prisha heard this, she said she wanted to work for Maher in Miraj. She took our one-year para-social worker training and worked at the Miraj Home for one and a half years. After that she said she couldn't handle the mentally disturbed (i.e. trauma-affected) women and asked to leave. So we shifted her to Maher's Priyata Home in the Vatsalydam Center near Pune. This Home is for mentally retarded women, (ie. mentally or physically affected from birth). Prisha worked there about one and a half years, both as a para-social worker and in the skill training department for crafts. Then she got sick. She decided she wanted to go home and stay with her parents. Now she is well and happy. She just completed a one-month Vipassana meditation course. At this course she met a man and they plan to marry. This man is from a very good and

Stories from Maher

wealthy family. Prisha's sister, Ruhi, told her that she will need to change her dress and her ways to fit with her fiancée's family!

Ruhi's story:

Ruhi was about fourteen when she came to Maher and she too had not been educated. She too attended an adult literacy program and, over three years, completed the exams for eighth, nineth and tenth standards. After this she wanted to do craft and tailoring training. Maher sent her to a special six-month craft training in Tamil Nadu with another Maher girl. An Italian friend of Maher sponsored both girls and paid all their fees and expenses. After this she worked in the Production Center. She was a hard worker. When she was twenty-one or two, she wanted to get married, so her mother arranged a marriage for her to a man from her village. The marriage was held in the village. Sister Lucy and I (Hira) traveled to attend the wedding.

After the marriage, Ruhi lived with her husband, but then she convinced him to come here to Maher. Her husband worked for Maher as a driver, and she worked as a housemother for about three or four years. Then they said they wanted to go back to the village and work the land. She and her husband planted grapes, wheat, and more. They have one son and one daughter who are going to school.

RISING TO NEW LIFE

Once part of the Maher family,
always part of the Maher family:
Eshana and her children have never forgotten Maher. Several of the children have now returned with their families to their village and are part of improving life in that village, including sharing about Maher.

Tharshan returned from working in the U.S. and founded Maher's Ex-Student Group for those who have "graduated" from Maher and wish to stay connected. He started a bank account to help Maher. He and many of these "graduates" contribute what they can all year. Then on Maher Day, all the money that has been collected that year is presented to Maher. This has ranged from 50,000 to 89,000 Indian rupees! [About $700-$1000 USD, a lot of money in India.]

Eshana sings the glory of Maher to any and everyone. In 2013, Eshana had the idea to felicitate [honor] Sister Lucy in her village. She invited her whole village, prepared food for all and, in front of all the village people, felicitated Sister Lucy.

[Later, Sister Lucy told this author that this honor touched her heart very deeply. By then, she had received over forty-one awards, yet she said "I count this felicitation more than all the other awards!"]

Ruhi and her whole family have really taken to heart

150

Stories from Maher

the Maher values. They are spreading these in the village, such as interfaith, caste-free, equal opportunities for women, and education for all children. And whenever Maher needs something, they come to help as much as they can. They are still poor—but they give whatever they can. For every rupee they earn they try to give one quarter to Maher! They bring food from their farm such as grapes or wheat flour: whatever they have they share with Maher.

On a recent overnight trip to Miraj, both Ruhi and her brother Achal came to visit. This is a several hour trip for them by bus, but they came in the evening after work. Rupali brought grapes from her vineyards to give to us. Achal could only stay long enough for tea, then had to go to Mumbai. He also gave a small cash donation to Maher. Ruhi stayed overnight and she and I (Hira) stayed up talking late into the night. The next morning, I wanted to give something to Ruhi, so I gave her some cloth to make clothes for her children, and some snacks. It was so wonderful to see her!

A Father's New Beginning Lifts the Whole Family: Suyash's Story
Narrated by Sister Lucy.

Suyash came to Maher in 2015. His condition was very bad: he was unable to speak, and he was too weak to even stand on his own. He was addicted to alcohol and tobacco. He had a wound on his leg which was not healing. We took him to Sassoon Hospital. The doctors informed us that he had diabetes. We started him on treatment.

He told us his wife was dead and he had three daughters taking shelter at another institution. He also had a sister nearby. He went to stay with her for one Diwali holiday. There he started to drink alcohol again. The wound in his leg worsened because he stopped taking the diabetes medicine.

He returned to Karunalaya, Maher's Men's Home, in a drunken state. Again, we took him to the hospital and they operated on his leg. Even after the surgery he could still not walk properly.

Suyash frequently asked us to take him to see his daughters. A social worker took him to the institution where the girls were, but they would not allow him to meet with his daughters. This happened three times. A few days later, this institution sent the three daughters to their grandmother's home permanently. They began to work as maids, though they were under-age.

About six months after this, the grandmother came to Maher with all three girls and told us that she had become unable to work due to her age and also because she had hypertension. She also told us no one had eaten in the last two days because they had no food in the house. Additionally, the landlord was asking for rent money which she didn't have. She asked that

Stories from Maher

Maher take them all in. Maher accepted all immediately. The girls were immediately enrolled in school.

Now slowly Suyash is changing and trying to become a good and kind person. He is working as a caretaker in Karunalaya Home. He is actively involved in everything. Two years after arriving at Maher the eldest daughter got married and is happily living with her husband.

Suyash is very happy and grateful to Maher for giving him and his family a secure and dignified life.

Chapter 7: The Fruits of Maher

This author sees, in the following group of young people, the "fruits" that have grown from Maher's care and nourishment. I see the literal future of Maher and of India in these amazing young men and women. All of them came to Maher as small children, some as orphans, some with their mother, and some boarding at Maher for the opportunities their families dreamed of for them. Some of them have continued at Maher as staff, whether as social workers or technological or administrative leaders. Some of them have taken good jobs outside Maher, in corporations, in Law, as leaders in their villages, or other roles. All are living Maher values in their everyday lives. They are in essence "home-grown" successors to Sister Lucy; they will help to assure that Maher's vision and values will live on even after Sister Lucy is no longer there to guide it. I am beyond impressed with each of these young people and hope that you will be too.

All of the stories below were told to me, or written in English, for this book. I have edited only for clarity and a bit of grammar, leaving some of the idiosyncrasies of a foreigner speaking English.

Stories from Maher

From "Untouchable" to Beloved "Brother" and Role Model at Maher: Mangesh's Story

I was born into a Dalit (Untouchable) caste family in a slum in Pune. There was no proper food, no proper shelter, no school. Life was brutal there. I have two older sisters. I never met my father, who beat my mother and sisters and even kicked my mother's belly when she was pregnant with me. She fled to her parents. She worked in a slum kindergarten as a cleaner to try to support us. My sisters also worked. During the week I sold sugarcane juice by the roadside looking for food to eat. One lady saw me on the road and asked me why I was not in school. She took me to Maher to meet Sister Lucy. I always say this is my Second Birth. I was seven years old when I first came to Maher with my mother's blessing.

Maher had only been in existence for three years then, with only one house and three staff members. At first it was hard, but then everyone became family. I never liked school because other kids hated me when they learned I was from the lower caste. I thought people at Maher would do the same thing if they got to know I am from lower caste. Maher put me in a Marathi-medium school. I had a school uniform. Every day I had enough food, my own blankets and so many other things: it was like a prayer answered! I caught up

155

quickly in school.

I liked the interfaith too where everyone respects all forms of God. I love meditation; I attended the ten-day Vipassana silence retreat after the ninth standard[27] and again after the twelfth standard. I love to dance, both Kathak and Bollywood. In addition to dancing, I play harmonium and *tabla,* (an Indian drum), and draw.

My studies in college led me to create a one-year project in Shirur district to study water usage in agriculture. Shirur village, about an hour from Vadhu Budruk, has about 20,000 people. I surveyed fifty homes. I taught the residents how to use water more effectively: how to filter it, how to store it, and how to use it efficiently in the fields. I successfully taught them how to measure groundwater and rainwater, and then to use that information to add water and increase crop results so they could earn more income. This project won awards at the college, university, and state levels.

I even traveled to Delhi for a national competition regarding this project. After the project was officially completed, I still traveled to the village, over an hour by bus each way, on my own time to help them. I knew that change takes time, and that if I would have stopped too soon, they would go back to the old ways.

During school and university, I continued with dance, drama and social awareness activities at

---

[27] This is much younger than most who attend.

Stories from Maher

Maher. I was selected for the President's Award from Delhi as a "Best Student of the Year" from among 870 colleges around India. This was a very proud moment for me. I dedicated this award to my two moms: one who gave me birth and one who is taking care of me, Sister Lucy Kurien. I was so amazed! As a boy who never thought he would go to school, now I am receiving the award from the President and UGC[28] head of India for overall best student.

After that I thought to work, but my mom said I should continue my studies. I decided to do an MBA. I received a full scholarship to do the MBA program at Pune University. It was very tough because previously classes had been in the Marathi local language and now classes were fully in English. Despite this, I also did very well and earned a Leadership Best Student award from the MBA program. I have a passion for learning and at the same time giving back to others in gratitude for what has been given to me.

As a young boy I got to travel to the U.K. with the Maher dancers. Inspired by this trip, I also later got selected as an International Peace Camp counselor to go to U.S., Africa, Nepal and Europe. My first trip to the U.S. I traveled with Sister Lucy and Gaus, another Maher boy. Gaus and I also did internships at a U.S.

---

[28] UGC is the University Grants Commission, a government body for the coordination, determination and maintenance of standards of teaching, examination and research in university education.

company at the end of this trip. I learned so much!

I am fully committed to Maher's values about interfaith and "love is my religion." When Sister Lucy was asked to speak at a conference on Interfaith Spirituality in Costa Rica, I went too and spoke as young leader from India. After this, I continued onto the U.S. for my second trip there as an ambassador for Maher. Another Maher girl, Soni, came also, her first trip to U.S.[29] I also got the opportunity to attend several Gender Reconciliation International[30] workshops, and then trained to be a facilitator for this work.

Given all these experiences, I decided to work full-time for Maher, the home where I learned basic human values and interfaith aspects of life. Working for Maher, I can share this to other communities. I am currently working with Maher as Youth Coordinator, Youth Ambassador, Trainer of Life Skills and International Interfaith Coordinator. In the latter role, I help spread the values of respect for different faiths in the communities and villages around Maher projects.

---

[29] This author watched how beautifully Mangesh mentored Soni during the above trip to the U.S. It was lovely to see how Mangesh had matured and could share his growing confidence in himself by nourishing the self-confidence of this shy young woman.

[30] This program originated in U.S. from Satyana Institute; it is now available in India and other international sites. Will Keepin and Cynthia Brix are the program founders. Several of the Maher young adults have attended and are becoming facilitators helping to suport the program to India.

Stories from Maher

All this was possible only because of the love, encouragement and support I received from Maher and the support of Friends of Maher around the world.

Coming to Maher As a Child, Remaining As a Social Worker: Vinayak's Story

My name is Vinayak Gade. I was born in Pune in 1994. My father was a painter and my mother was a housewife. Our family was poor. Then my mom and dad were blessed with a girl child, my younger sister, whom I love very much. We both attended school in a Marathi government school in Fhursungi village, in Pune District.

My father started selling illegal liquor, and my family situation totally changed. My father began to drink a lot of alcohol and started so many issues in the family. He got involved with bad people and started hitting my mother and I. One night my father hit my mother a lot and she left home. I was alone for three days without food. During these three days I sold plates with flowers, coconuts and Haldi Kumkum[31] in front of a temple. Then my mother came back.

After this my father married a second woman and

---

[31] Haldi Kumkum are the red and yellow powders used in Hindu ceremonies.

RISING TO NEW LIFE

the domestic violence got worse, so my mother decided to leave the home, taking my sister and I with her. She took us to my grandparent's house in Pune. My mother and father had made a love marriage and it was not accepted by my mother's family, so they would not take us in.

Just before this, we had learned that both my mother and father were HIV positive. My mother became so sick, we admitted her to a hospital in Wagholi, just outside Pune. It was here we learned about Maher. My mother brought me and my sister to Maher in 2002. I was eight years old. Later that same year, both of my parents died; my sister and I became orphans. Then in 2018, my sister died. She was living at Maher with me and we were very close. I still miss her very much.

My life completely changed when I came to Maher. I was a very naughty boy at first, but I started going to school and enjoyed all the activities at Maher: dance, sports, singing and drawing.

I got the chance to be part of the Maher dance group and the drama group. In 2007, we went to the U.K. and performed over thirty shows in different parts of England. We also performed a drama about Gandhi's life. We saw many amazing sights and ate new, strange, food.

I completed my tenth standard, then did my diploma to become an electrician. Next, I completed University

Stories from Maher

and earned a Bachelor of Arts in Geography. Then I attended the Youth Leadership Diploma Program in Centre for Youth Development and Activities, a big NGO in India.

Now I am working in Maher Pune Office as an Office Assistant while I am working on my MSW. Starting in summer 2021, I have the opportunity to do one year volunteering in Germany through Red Cross and Vollanta. In preparation, I completed my first level of German language study.[32]

I am really thankful to Didi and my Maher family for all they have done for me. Now my dream is to give back and help Maher's mission.

From Poverty to Finance Professional: Surekha's Story

I came to Maher with my mother when I was eight years old. My mother is blind in one eye. We were very poor and didn't have support from anyone. My mother came to know about Maher and so we came here. We quickly settled in. I started school and my mother began working as a housemother.

In Maher I got so many wonderful opportunities. I

---

[32] Vollanta program offers a one-year exchange for young people from India to volunteer in Germany, and for German young people to volunteer in India, whom Maher regularly hosts. Despite COVID, Vinayak travelled to Germany to begin this program.

got to get a full education. I got to take part in different activities like dance, drama, sports, and *tabla* classes.

In 2007, I was part of the group of Maher children who traveled to England to perform Indian Classical Dance called Kathak. I continued to study dance and specialize in Kathak for many years. I performed in other states such as Jharkhand and Kerala, and in Delhi. After I completed twelfth standard, I traveled to other Maher centers to teach dance to Maher children. I continued teaching dance even while attending University.

Maher gave me so much support, helping me to grow in many ways. As college and university students, Sister Lucy had many of us, both girls and boys, "emcee" the many programs and events that Maher frequently hosted. This helped me to stand in front of many people, and feel confident speaking at large events, first at Maher, and then elsewhere. Sister Lucy and Maher always encouraged me, telling me that I could do anything.

I worked with Kapoor Foundation, a Canadian NGO, as a Project Manager in India. Each year, Kapoor Foundation hosted competitions for young people who had to design and complete projects in Science, Technology, Engineering or Math. My role was both like a coach to help the young people design their projects, but also to make sure every project was completed and turned in on time. This was a wonderful opportunity

Stories from Maher

and I earned "Best Project Manager Award" from Kapoor Foundation in 2012.

My dream: first I want to become a professional and a good person. Then I want to become the best finance manager I can and work with an international company.

And just like Maher helped me, I would like to support those children who have no one to take care of them. I want to help them get a good education and help them to be something in their life. I owe my wonderful life to Maher.

Note: Surekha recently completed her MBA and now has a wonderful job in Finance at HDFC Bank.

A Girl-child Demonstrates Her Value and Her Gifts: Poonam's Story

My family hails from Uttar Pradesh (UP) but for the past twenty-five years we have been living in Pune, Maharashtra. My mother and father got married in UP; it was a love marriage. My father belonged to a Rajput (Hindu) family and my mother was from a fishermen family. Therefore their marriage was not acceptable in my father's home and his family turned their back on him. My parents came to Pune. and they started living a happy life. I am the oldest child and I have a younger brother and sister.

After some years, my father got cancer. He passed away when I was in seventh standard. It was a shocking moment for us. We had never gone to my father's home; we didn't know any information about his family. My father had never told us his family's address, so it was not possible to find my father's family.

My mother was very young when she got married to my father; she doesn't even know her own surname. She knows only the name which my father gave to her. She was never educated. When he passed away, we didn't have any savings; we were penniless. Some neighbors and my father's friends came together and collected money and then performed my father's final rites.

After my father's death, our condition became worse because we were living in a shambled house with leaks in the roof and no sanitation. My mother was the only working member in our family. Sometimes we didn't even have enough food to eat or enough clothes to wear. After my father's passing, we did not celebrate any festival because we didn't have money.

When my father was sick, one Sister always came to pray for him. Her name was Sister Libiya. Then one year after my father's death, Sister Libiya came to my life like an angel and took me to a heaven called Maher, where I met God and her name is Sister Lucy Kurien, our Didi. (My siblings came too.) My life began

Stories from Maher

changing from that moment onward. I got an education, food, shelter, love, care, respect, and the confidence to take my life forward.

When I was at Maher in twelfth standard, my mother got remarried to another person. He cheated my mother and left her when she was nine months pregnant. It was a very painful and depressing time for me and my family. We all suffered a lot because of societal humiliation and abuses, but because of Maher's love, care and support I got over them. Now I don't have any shameful feelings about this time. Now I have another younger half sister; she is very dear to us all. She brings great joy and laughter to our lives. My mother is still living outside Maher, but if she needs anything, Maher is always the first one to reach out to her.

I received many precious gifts from my experiences and Maher. Dance is one of my favorite "gifts." I learned "Kathak" (classical Indian dance) in Maher and successfully passed four exam levels. I got the chance to teach dance to other children at different centers of Maher. I also performed dances on big stages, at companies and festivals, which was a great opportunity for me. I helped write and perform in "street plays" for education in the villages on various social topics.

In addition to dance and drama, we had lots of opportunities to develop creative and leadership skills.

I learned "Warily"[33] painting in Production at Maher. I also helped organize Maher's annual Sports Camps for four years in a row in collaboration with other Maher peers. Each Sports Camp lasts one week and is for several hundred children.

I had many educational opportunities too. While I was still in high school, I got the chance to study at Aurangabad Holy Cross convent. Through this I got opportunities to go to Goa, Kerala, Hyderabad, Mumbai, and many companies. I gained exposure to more of the world, including exploring the culture and values of other states. After tenth standard I got to take a class in Computer Science. I graduated from B.I.S. College with first class in chemistry specialization. Later I attended Pune University and earned a bachelor's degree in Chemistry. I was invited to be part of several programs and trainings, including Gender Reconciliation.

For post-graduate studies, I won admission to Sadhana Centre for Management and Leadership Development. There I met many people of various backgrounds, skills, and knowledge, and learned many things. This was a management and leadership course where we had similar subjects to an MBA program where we got a chance to learn and enhance our leadership qualities. My specialization was in Human

---

[33] Warily is a tribal, stylized form of painting that decorates many handmade Maher Production Center items.

Stories from Maher

Resource Management where I got deep knowledge about recruitment, training and development, employee engagement, and Corporate Social Responsibility (CSR) activities. I learned business software, such as Excel, Word, and PowerPoint. This program also gave me the chance to improve upon my English knowledge and general awareness.

For the leadership qualities we put our foot forward for initiatives such as arranging convocations, planning CSR activities and an initiative for a blood donation camp. Another example was Swachh Bharat Abhiyan. Here we cleaned the college area and campaigned for the same as a part of "Clean India."[34]

Currently I am in Pune with my birth family. I got diagnosed with TB and was not well for a year. I have been resting the whole last year and looking for a new job opportunity.

In spring 2021 I will marry Yogesh Bohr, another Maher boy. (His story follows.)

My three siblings, one brother and two sisters, all are younger than me. We were all raised at Maher. My sister Yashoda got married to a Christian boy and they have a boy child of seven months. My brother got

---

[34] Swachh Bharat Abhiyan's mission is to bring Hygienics, the science concerned with the prevention of illness and maintenance of health, through cleansing, sanitation & scavenging, using modern equipment, processes and/or technologies.

RISING TO NEW LIFE

married to a Muslim girl six months back and my youngest half-sister is studying in fifth standard. I have deliberately written the religion because this is what Maher's interfaith value is: love is our religion.

I really want to give thanks to our whole Maher family and especially our Didi. She is always with me. She has always guided me and shown me the best path for me. Dealing with me was not a cakewalk for Didi because I was so stubborn. I was going through so much mental pressure due to my family condition, but she always held me in her wings and gave me so much love, care, and hope to live a better life. And now here I am doing great in my life! My Maher youth is a part of my life that I shall always cherish. I love you Didi.

Once an Orphan, Now a Homeowner and Trustee of Maher: Yogesh's Story

My family lived in Mumbai. We had our own small house. My father was an alcoholic and in 2000 he died. I was in fourth standard. After this my mother had to take care of me and my two brothers.

In 2002, my mother died. This was so sad for us. (I was in sixth standard.) Even though we had our house, it was very hard to take care of ourselves without a mother and father. Ever since I was small, I would go everywhere with my mother; I was never alone. How

Stories from Maher

were we to survive?

My uncle and grandfather lived near Kendur, a small village near Vadhu Center. My younger brother Nandu and I went to live with him. By this time our oldest brother was eighteen, so he was on his own in Mumbai. Uncle had three children of his own, two boys and a girl. Kendur was so small then that there were no school facilities. We sat outside with no chairs or desks; one teacher taught all subjects. This was strange for us because, in Mumbai, we went to a big school with all the facilities. And we were missing our mother a lot too. Because no one at this "school" made us attend classes, instead we roamed around outside. Uncle and Grandfather were very upset by this. How long could they keep caring for two more children? It was hard for them too.

They came to know about Maher. One day Uncle came to Maher and he spoke with Hiratai. He told her about his family and us, his nephews. He inquired about admission. He came home and told us what he had learned and what he was thinking. Uncle wanted help with all the children. But Maher said no, that he should keep his three children with him, families are best living together. Uncle was unsure about splitting up us cousins. But Grandfather wanted us to continue school if we wanted. He made the decision we should go to Maher so we could continue a good education like we had started in Mumbai.

By this time, we had been with Uncle one year. We had begun to feel less sad about missing our mother and we missed school. Both of us are very good in studies. But we had essentially missed one full year of school since what little we had in Kendur barely counted.

One day Uncle and Grandfather told us we will go to school again. They purchased uniforms, school bags, some clothing for us and took us to Maher who admitted us. I remember my first day here. I was in seventh standard and Nandu in fifth standard. At this time, there were only forty or fifty school age children at Maher. That first day, the whole day, we were crying. We missed our family. We sat out by Maher's gate looking for any people from Uncle's village to ask them to take us home again.

Didi, Hira, Nishikant [a social worker] ... everyone was talking to us. Sister Monica was there too. Everyone was telling us this will be a good life and we will get to go to school. They gave us bicycles to ride. This made us a little happier.

I started into high school which in India is eighth standard. I was the first Maher boy to go to high school; the other boys were younger and were in primary schools. But there were five Maher girls also going also to high school so we six went together.

It was hard for me. From a small family with mother and two brothers, to now such a big family at Maher. I

Stories from Maher

am emotional and I feel everything. I cannot forget the past easily. Initially I was still thinking "How will we survive? How will we do this? What will happen to us?" But slowly with all the love and attention from Didi and staff who took care of us ... I cannot explain in words.

After I finished eighth standard, I totally forgot my worries. Now Maher was my family. The men, like Nishikant, they took care of me like a father would. Didi, the housemothers, they care for me like my mother would. All the love and affection was so nice. I stopped missing my mom.

After eighth standard they took a group of us boys to live at Shirur house for ninth through twelfth standard.[35] In tenth standard I got the highest percentage in my class.

After twelfth standard I told Didi that I wanted to study engineering. Didi was so happy. She wanted Maher children to be doctors, engineers, nurses, policemen, pharmacists, everything. In those days engineering study was not easy because there were lots of expenses for this school. I wondered how Maher would do this. Didi said: "Yogesh, I am your mother. It is my duty to provide for you. Don't you worry. Just keep studying hard and earning good grades. Be a good example to others."

For next three years, I attended diploma courses at

---

[35] By law, Maher cannot keep boys older than twelve in the same Home as girls. The Maher Home in Shirur is all boys.

JSPM College, a Jesuit college in Wagholi. I graduated from here with "80% with distinction" and a Diploma in Electronics and Telecommunications Engineering. Then I studied three more years for my bachelor's in the same.

Through all my schooling I had all the opportunities at Maher. Maher's taekwondo classes started in Shirur when I was there. Maher won lots of awards in the local competitions for taekwondo. We also had *tabla*, drawing, and singing classes at Maher too. Even computer classes. I also performed in the Gandhi street dramas, teaching the example of Gandhi in the villages. I did some of Maher dance classes, but dance was not so interesting to me as taekwondo, especially when I was younger. When I got older, I also taught some of the taekwondo classes to the smaller children. Then in engineering school we didn't have as much time and were focused on studies.

I know if I had been in my family home, I could never have dreamed this. We could not have afforded this quality of education. Not just the school itself, but everything else I was learning at Maher: the interfaith, the respect for myself and all people, the dance, the values we are getting, even the prayers. I don't think many people, even those living with families, get this quality of education. I am so very grateful.

Even when I was in eighth through tenth standard, I tutored other Maher children in math. I helped them

Stories from Maher

prepare for exams. This was good for me too. It grew my confidence in myself, as well as my attachment with the younger children of my Maher family. These children, when they had difficulties, they could come talk to me about anything.

Later, from college, I got to help arrange and manage the Sports Camps for the smaller Maher children. This is such a good opportunity to learn leadership, organization and planning, all while managing several hundred children.

I also got the chance to represent Maher at "International Peace Camp" in Africa. I had asked for a couple years to go to U.S. with Didi but I never got that chance because I could not get a U.S. visa. But I got the Africa visa, so this was my chance to travel outside India. Mangesh, Gaus and I all went together. It was a fabulous experience for us. Ten days we were in Uganda for International Peace Camp at an orphan school there. Gretchen-Auntie took us.[36] It was such good exposure for us. We got to see how the people live, experience their customs and to see the poverty there. So much we learned.

After I completed my engineering degree, Sister

---

[36] Gretchen Rowe is the founder and Director of Peace Camp International at Interfaith Community Sanctuary in Seattle, WA. They hold International Peace Camps in U.S. and Africa. Several of the Maher young people have attended over the years as both campers and counselors.

Lucy told me it was time for me to go outside Maher to work. But I wanted to work at Maher, at least for one year. I worked in Pune office that year. I arranged programs, youth camps, tuitions for the children, things like that.

For Sister Lucy's sixtieth birthday and Maher's 20th Anniversary we wanted to do something special that would make her very happy. We got the idea to prepare a photo gallery. The photo gallery showed all Didi's life. We had to work on it in secret, so we did it in the garage at Vatsalydam. We worked so hard, sometimes sixteen hours in one day to get it ready. Then, on the day, we had such a heavy rain! It poured! We were so worried how do we transport it without damaging it. But amazingly none of the photos in the photo gallery were damaged! When Didi saw it for the first time she cried.

As I was helping to make this, I was reviewing too the whole Maher journey, I was reflecting and remembering. All these skills we have thanks to Maher.

We had to learn time management and delegation too. We had so many projects going on, especially as we got older. All the children wanted to be a part of everything. So older children like me, who were managing many of these projects, with staff support, had to choose who can do what tasks. And we still had to manage our studies. It was always a lot! Now I can do anything. Anyone tells me to do something, I can figure it out! And I work very hard all day. At Maher it

Stories from Maher

was always something: painting, cleaning, anything. We learned not to rely on "someone else." This is how Didi brought us up, to face any situation in life. That is happiness.

Then Didi told me it was time for me to go outside Maher and work. She wanted all of us to have "real world" experience beyond Maher. She wanted us to learn what it is like on the outside, without Didi and staff looking out for us, knowing what was good for us and what was not. She told us that corporate culture would be very different. This would be a learning experience.

Chaya Pamula, a Maher Trustee, has her company, PamTen, in Hyderabad. It is an international software firm, headquartered in New Jersey in the U.S. My brother Nandu was already working there as a software engineer. Chaya said Gaus and I could also come work for her there. The thirtieth of November was our last day at Maher. I remember that day so clearly. The whole day again I was crying! This time I was crying because I had to leave Maher. I am laughing now as I recall this! Maher arranged a farewell program for Gaus and I. We were both crying. I didn't know I had so much water in me! Didi was also crying. We knew we were still part of Maher, we were just going out to work; but we were still so sad.

I have worked here as a software engineer for almost two years. I have had many new experiences.

175

Rising to New Life

For example, in a company we have set working hours, eight hours a day. There is a spreadsheet tool we must complete, where I log exactly how much time I spend on each task I do, accounting for all forty hours every week. Didi never did anything like that. We can't challenge this; we just do it. This is a skill to know how I am spending my time, using it better. It helps us plan.

Didi likes to hear how we are, what we are doing and any suggestions from us based on what we learn from working outside. For example, at PamTen, we use email to communicate with co-workers about projects, deadlines, who does what, etc. At Maher we just have conversations. I have been thinking, what if we did more on email at Maher? Then there is a record, you can look back at it if you forget, or if people remember the conversation differently. Of course the office uses a lot of email, but not so much other staff.

In Hyderabad there were people with lots of schooling and high salaries, but I felt more lucky. After work, they just lay around and played; they didn't really have anything else to do, they didn't contribute to society. But I was always working on planning something for Maher: Sports Camp, International Children's Day, Maher Day ... there is always something. We are very attached to Maher—we don't forget the values and our family, even though we live a long way away now. It's a long journey from Hyderabad to Pune, about thirteen hours on the train one way, but

Stories from Maher

we come back often on the train for holidays and even weekends.

It's a wonderful experience for us. When I finished my Engineering degree, I wanted to work at Maher, with Didi. There is so much satisfaction from working at Maher. At night, you fall asleep satisfied with what you are doing. It's not that there is not satisfaction in my work outside—I am earning money, gaining knowledge and skills, that satisfaction is there. But it's not the same. When we are working with the children, affecting their lives, nothing can compare with this.

After two years at PamTen, my brother Nandu got an even better job offer at another international company, Accentia Technologies, also in Hyderabad. It is a big multinational IT services company, one of the largest in India. Recently Nandu was shifted to their Pune office.

We are both still deeply connected to Maher. We see how busy Didi is now. We want to help her. This is why my brother Nandu and I bought a small plot of the land adjacent to Vadhu Center and are building a house. A few other staff bought small plots here too. It's like such a dream—from nothing to now owning a piece of land and building a house. All things like this happen only because of Maher and Didi. I am proud to join the Maher Trustees and to further serve Maher. I am the first Trustee raised at Maher.

I am thinking that later this year, once the house is

RISING TO NEW LIFE

ready, that I would like to marry. I do not have a girlfriend. I will speak to Didi and to my Uncle; they will find me someone.

The love from Maher and everyone—that completely changed our lives. Both my brother and I. Now when we go to visit Uncle in his village, all the people are so proud of us. They say Yogesh, even without a mother or a father you completed your studies.

It's a dream; my life now is a dream come true.

This author checked in with Yogesh recently. Due to COVID, Yogesh has returned to Pune, though he continues his IT job at PamTen, working remotely. Their house is finished. It's lovely, complete with a garage and car. After this, Yogesh got married to another Maher girl, Poonam (whose story is also included here). It's easier this way since they understand each other and the Maher values.

From Orphan to Scholarship to Degree in Psychology from U.S. University: Ravina's Story.

I was five years old when my father passed away, and soon after that grandpa died too. My twin sisters were three years old. After these deaths, my mother's support system collapsed and she was on her own with us three small girls.

178

Stories from Maher

My widowed mother is my first inspiration. Coming from a rural background she did not complete tenth standard. She married my dad when she was about nineteen years old. She always made sure that I and my younger two sisters understood that, no matter what, our education came first. My mother was determined we girls would be educated. She worked hard, often more than one job at a time, all to provide for my sisters and me. She worked in sugar cane and peanut farms, plus as a janitor in my primary school and in a local bank. Our poor but loving family was everything to me.

Then my mother became very ill. I was the primary caregiver, with some help from my mom's parents. My younger sisters did what they could. I bathed her, fed her, gave her medicines, and did everything I could to save her. Then on May 28, 2008, I lost my mother. Usually, I cry a lot. But that one moment I remember that I didn't cry, because I became my sisters' mom. I performed all the rituals for my mom, just like a son. I was in shock. I was waiting for someone to pinch me and tell me it was a dark nightmare. But my thirteen-year-old heart knew that it was time for me to grow up so that my sisters and I could not only survive but thrive in this world. My sisters were only eleven years old.

My mother left me with three important lessons:
    1. Education—never give up

Rising to New Life

2. As siblings, stay together wherever we go
3. Self-respect, hard work and integrity will bring us a long way

I was determined we three girls would remain together. No one in our family could afford to take all three of us. We toured several orphanages but couldn't find one that felt safe for three young girls. Finally, our neighbor told us about Maher. My siblings, neighbors, my uncle, and my grandpa from mother's side all went to visit Maher. The first thing I saw was the sign, "Maher—Rising to New Life." It includes the image of a shadow of a mother holding the hand of a child as they walk together on their journey into the bright light. My heart said, "Yes, this is the place for us." My uncle hugged us and cried with us. He felt in his heart that if only he was rich, he could have kept us with my cousin-sisters and my aunt in their house. However, it was the right decision to go to Maher.

Our transition in Maher was tough: overnight we went from being in a small family to living with twenty-five children in one house. Slowly, my sisters and I learned to do the daily chores. We began to follow schedules. I looked around me and listened to other children who felt safe to share their stories. Listening to inspiring stories of people reminded me that there were children who had seen worse than I. I began to be grateful for my own journey.

Stories from Maher

At Maher I became very reserved. I kept to myself, my sisters, my chores, my studies, and extracurricular activities such as Kathak dance and Indian classical music. Every day, I focused on my mother's big dreams for us. Every day I took a deep breath and told myself we are safe, loved, cared for and I am one step closer to fulfilling my, and my mother's, dreams. Maher taught me to be disciplined, independent, empathetic, and hopeful.

I had great teachers who recognized my potential and guided me to be the best version of myself. At Maher, housemothers and social workers supported me to excel in school. After tenth standard I enrolled in V.S. Satav college for further education in the field of science. I also started teaching Kathak classes every Saturday and Sunday at Maher's Apti center, a small village near Vadhu. That money was used as college traveling money. English was my biggest challenge.

In 2013, Maher learned about United World College (UWC) and that there was a UWC center in Pune.[37] Seven teenagers from Maher went to visit UWC along with Sister Lucy. A Maher boy and I were selected through a written application process. Next were in-

---

[37] UWC is an international network of schools and educational programs with the shared aim of "making education a force to unite people, nations and cultures for peace and a sustainable future".

person interviews, in English. The Maher staff helped me prepare.

I had studied English since I was in the first standard, but in Marathi-medium public schools. This does not prepare one for conversation in English. During the interview I cried and I said I want to discuss this in Hindi. I told them this language (English) was hiding my knowledge because language is the only way we human beings communicate. I argued that what I think about a particular issue is the important part and will help them to recognize my personality and my courage. Finally, I got permission to give my answers in Hindi. One of the teachers came behind my chair and said, "Congratulations Ravina!" I was the first Maher student selected to this program, and on a full scholarship.

I found that I was the least privileged among the students at UWC, and all of them were more proficient in English. I had to catch up to match other people's language abilities as well as earn good grades. This was a residential school, so I was away from Maher and my sisters for the first time. I was with people from all over India and the world. I began to understand global views and people's ways of life. I had brilliant teachers who were patient with me. I studied psychology, biology, math, and dance. I always did my best. Many times, I would study until four in the

Stories from Maher

morning. I felt I had to excel so that other kids from Maher would get this chance in the future.

After graduation from UWC, I received a full four-year Davis Scholarship and Westminster Grant to Westminster College, in Missouri, USA. I was the first student from Maher to study abroad. May 11, 2019, was a very proud moment when Sister Lucy watched me walk down the aisle with a diploma for Bachelors of Arts and Sciences with a major in Psychology and a minor in Education. We shared many happy tears. My sisters saw me achieve what my mother dreamed for us.

In the USA, I got connected to Maher supporters who later became my mentors and friends; they supported me and hosted me during my summer and winter breaks. I would love to name them all, but do not have space here.

Since my graduation, I have been working as an Advocate Case Manager for the Women's Center for Advancement in Omaha, Nebraska, United States. I serve survivors (men and women) of domestic abuse, sexual assault, human trafficking, stalking, and harassment. My current work inspires me to become a clinical counselor.

My dream is to get accepted to a Master of Clinical Counseling program in the U.S. and earn my therapist license so that I can open a private counseling practice and help people with their mental health healing

RISING TO NEW LIFE

journey. In the future, I want to be able offer free counseling sessions to support the women, men, and students in Maher with their healing, so that they can persevere and thrive. As Sister Lucy says, "Whatever you do in your career, make sure to touch as many lives as possible with your gifts." I also want to decrease cultural stigma around mental health in south Asian cultures.

I was also able to help my sisters get sponsorship in the U.S. through the Nebraska-based Maher Friends group. Both my sisters have been studying in the U.S. for two-and-a-half years now. My mother is looking down at us, thanking Sister Lucy for continuing the mother role. I imagine her enjoying the moment of seeing us reunited in the U.S. again. It's hard to think now that I came from nothing really, when I began this journey.

I am grateful to Sister Lucy Kurien, the founder of Maher, to have lived experiences and life lessons at Maher. I am grateful that I had a strong mother who still lives in my heart. I am grateful to my family and all my mentors and teachers in India and in the U.S. I am grateful to my younger sisters who trusted me and my decisions at a very young age.

When people see me now, they would never know where I came from or how far I have traveled. My success is the fruit of my determination, resilience, intelligence, perseverance, hard work, and my intuitive gifts. I want to share this story so that anyone reading it receives the message that if I was able to get this far, they can too.

Maher College-going girls teaching dance to some of the younger girls.

RISING TO NEW LIFE

Curiosity, Talent and Determination:
Amol's Story

In 1997, Maher was in its first year, with no staff besides Sister Lucy, no money. Maher was already "full" when Amol's mother came with five children, three girls, two boys, all under the age of ten. Sister Lucy took them all in. Here is Amol's story from coming to Maher up to today—twenty-three years later.

Our family was very poor and homeless. We could not even afford a daily meal for the family. My parents worked as day laborers on a construction site. One day, while carrying a heavy loads of bricks, my mother fell on her stomach and got hurt. The family had no money to take her for any medical care. A big tumour or something began to grow. The tumour was getting bigger and bigger and she felt she was about to die.

Someone told her about Sister Lucy. The very next day she took all of us five children to Maher for shelter. Maher had no Home for men at this time, so my father continued working. Maher paid for my mother to have surgery, saving her life. After she recovered, she began to work in Maher helping to care for other women and children. When we children were old enough, we began to attend the local school. As Maher developed other programs, things like dance, taekwondo and art, we all took part.

Stories from Maher

Among my three sisters, the second one was handicapped. Maher paid for her treatment. My eldest sister got married when she was very young. The two other sisters studied until the twelfth grade and then got married. Now they all are well settled.

In 2004 our father abandoned the family. Until then he visited us at Maher. Later, when we needed him, he was not there.

I was five years old when my mother and our family came to Maher. I started school and proved to be a bright student. When I began fifth standard, Sister Lucy sent me to Father Agnel's Multipurpose School, a boarding school in Mumbai. Here I started playing soccer. Soccer was the only thing that helped me forget my worries. I forgot my trauma and wholeheartedly got involved in the game. I was good and was selected for the school team. I participated in many tournaments at the state and national levels through the tenth standard.

Each year India's Slum Soccer organization arranges state and national level tournaments in different places in India. I participated on the Maher Team as captain. In 2010 I received the Best Soccer Player Award in the tournament between Maher and HSBC International Bank.

Through these games, I was selected to play on the Indian National Slum Soccer Team. This is one achievement of which I am very proud. As part of the

RISING TO NEW LIFE

Indian team, I travelled to Poznan, Poland in 2013 to compete in the Homeless Soccer World Cup. This event was for homeless youth from all over the world. It was a wonderful experience to travel to Poland and meet the other children. I was proud to have been selected and my Maher family was very happy. This was my first time outside India. To this day, I continue my love of soccer by coaching the current Maher team.

One event in my childhood that stood out was in 2005 when I was eleven years old. A friend of Maher, Mr. Preetam, came for a visit. He brought a toy electric boat to be assembled and he wanted to give it as a gift to a child in Maher. He asked Sister Lucy to recommend a child who had the capability to completely assemble this electric boat. Sister Lucy recommended me! I was thrilled to receive the assignment, though I never understood what Sister Lucy had seen in me to choose me for this wonderful project. Preetam-Uncle (as I used to call him, out of fondness) said he expected me to complete the assignment in one month. I accepted the challenge and started work on the boat.

As the project progressed, I lost all track of time; I even lost track of day and night. I gave it my all and used all my time for the task. I felt a passion I had never felt before. I completed the fully electric, working boat in three days flat! This feat impressed everyone in Maher. This helped to grow my motivation and

188

Stories from Maher

confidence. Through this incident, I learned more about myself and realized my potential.

Another part of growing up that shaped me came from watching cartoons. As a young boy, I used to watch the Walt Disney cartoon *Tom & Jerry*. It was my first cartoon. After watching, I started making cartoon drawings. Later, in the Father Agnel School, I never got to watch cartoons because the older boys preferred to watch movies, both Hollywood and Bollywood. During computer class one of my friends and I used to search for information on the movies such as how they were made and what kind of software they used for the effects. We studied them for hours.

This led me to ponder more seriously what my future could be, what I wanted to do in life. I was always good at painting as well. I realized if I followed all my passions, I could truly be successful in life, overcoming all the trauma of my past. A friend suggested that I could do very well in animation. I researched and learned that the most important skills included drawing and design, as well as visualization and knowledge of the color wheel and color theory, plus computer skills. I knew this was my path. I dreamed of working for Disney or Pixar because they are the best in the field. I wanted to do a Bachelor of Fine Arts (BFA) in animation and digital art. It turns out Pune is the up and coming place for design, so I could study right here. Thanks to Maher, I completed my diploma in

RISING TO NEW LIFE

Multimedia from Design Maniac Studio School in Pune.

Even before my BFA, in my free time I started modelling Maher construction projects (3D elevation). I worked on this in collaboration with the architect who plans Maher projects. He provided me the AutoCAD plans, which I used to create interior and exterior models in 3ds Max.

While in school I worked part-time at Maher helping with all things computer. After graduation, I accepted Sister Lucy's offer to work full-time at Maher. My job is Computer Design Manager for the Maher centers. My job responsibilities include configuration and maintenance of all the computers, printers, networks, software and technology. I design and manage the website and social media accounts. When COVID arrived and we began on-line learning for the children and virtual events on ZOOM, I arranged all this too.

Additionally, I am responsible for the photography of Maher events. I travel with Sister Lucy to attend events, take photographs and use them in designing newsletters, brochures, banners, the website, and all the other social media posts. I have always enjoyed photography. In 2013, one of my photos was selected in the Jaipur Photography Exhibition. I was one of eighty-five photographers selected out of 1500 entrants from all over India.

I also continue Maher's tradition of volunteering. I am a member of the advisory board of Global

Stories from Maher

Opportunity Youth Network (GOYN).[38] We work with young people aged fifteen to twenty-nine who are out of school, unemployed, or working in informal jobs.

For me, getting educated is very important, as no one in my family has ever had an opportunity to pursue higher education. I would like to render my services to other children in society who never got an opportunity to study and who are suffering because of poverty. I also want to help Maher; because of Maher, my life had become a new and better life. I hope to inspire other Maher children to follow their dreams by showing them that I have followed my own.

Recently I got married. This was a love and inter-caste marriage, which is rare in India. We have our own home now outside Maher and we all are living happily along with my parents. My mother is still working in Maher, and happily my father returned to the family. I am proud that I can fulfill Indian cultural expectations that a son help care for his aging parents.

---

[38] GOYN is a "global initiative catalyzing systems shifts for youth opportunity in communities around the world through the creation of sustainable training, employment and income-earning pathways.

RISING TO NEW LIFE

Baby Girl Comes to Maher, Grows into a Maher "Ambassador": Soni's Story

Excerpted from a two-hour conversation with Soni.

I was very small when my mother left my father. My father did his best to care for me. It was really difficult for him since I was so small and a girl. We were living on the street; we had no shelter and no food.

A woman in our neighborhood told my father about Maher and so he brought me here. He did not stay. Maher had no home for men at that time. The only men here were social workers. Plus, without needing to take care of a baby girl, he could work. He came to visit whenever he could.

I was about three years old when I came to Maher. When I first came, I was so afraid and crying and crying, not knowing where I was. Didi and Hiratai loved me and I became happy. Didi is like my other mother. She is so kind. Maher took good care of me, gave me a good education, and good values too. I started school in Marathi-medium and did well. I completed basic school and went on to eleventh and twelfth standard. I got good grades.

Maher gives us so many extra classes we can take: singing, drawing, painting, dance, taekwondo, computers, everything! This is more than I could get even if I were living in a normal family.

Stories from Maher

When I was in the fourth standard, I joined dance classes. We learned Kathak Indian Classical Dance and I still take dance classes. I have passed six levels of Kathak. I also do Bollywood dance too. I love to dance! I teach dance now to the children in different Pune Homes.[39]

I got the chance to audition for "IGT: India Got Talent". I traveled to Mumbai for this. It was difficult and I was nervous, but it was a good experience. Maher teaches us to compete to grow ourselves. All the world is a competition and so we must learn to push ourselves to learn, grow and to survive in the world. Maher helps us develop courage and feelings of strength to stand on our own feet.

After tenth and twelfth standard completions, I got to participate in Maher's Youth Camp. Staff, plus some of the older Maher grown up children, organize this camp for us. It is good to have fun at these times because in these years you are focusing on your career, on work and don't have time for things like this anymore. So many things I learned there, like cooking and sewing. We also learned more crafts and even more dancing. All the children share their life

---

[39] Note: this author got to see a group of very small girls (about five- or six-year-olds) that Soni taught as they performed a Bollywood dance at a Maher program. It was lovely to watch Soni encouraging them and helping them to have fun while also performing!

experiences—a different kind of bonding for us, different than when studying hard. And each share their stories with the group: some have really sad stories, some happier. We listen, and we didn't know, even though they are our Maher brothers and sisters. Each person is a hero in their own life story. It's like that. Really amazing. I am always thinking—oh I want to learn from that person!

I believe because of Maher I can do anything. Now I am in my second of three years of college, pursuing a degree in Business and Communication. I am interested in banking and accounting. I am enjoying it. So many good experiences I got in Maher! I am thinking I am such a lucky, lucky person that I got this Maher family! My Maher family is huge and so lovely. All the staff are so lovely.

What is different about growing up at Maher?

We often don't get chances in Indian society for education, let alone the extras like dance. Especially in the villages, the girls don't have rights even for education.[40] At Maher, girls and boys get equal rights to everything. That is one of Maher's values. Also "love is my religion." These values are some of the first things I learned at Maher. It's a good thing for India because now there are all the religious fights going on.

---

[40] The right to education exists on paper, but no one enforces this, so culture is what determines who gets educated.

Stories from Maher

Every child and staff practices "love is my religion."

I talk about this to my friends at school and they are getting inspired by "love is my religion" and now they too are practicing this!

Gender equity is another Maher value. In India until now there has not been much gender equity for girls and boys. They are always saying no, girls can't do this or that. Only boys. But in Maher all the children can do all things.

Didi is always saying "Beta[41], you can do it!" If I am ever discouraged, Didi is encouraging me. When I was first in the U.S. and I could not speak English well at all, I was so scared. She said "No, Beta you can do it! Just keep going with the flow. You will learn." She is so positive. And her hands—it's like someone is giving me energy! And so then I feel "Yes I can do it!" And I did! Of course, I must still practice my English and keep learning!

The experience in the U.S. was an awesome experience for me in my life. Because of Didi and Maher I got this chance. It was a golden opportunity for me. We started in Costa Rica at an Interfaith Spirituality Conference. Sister Lucy was a speaker. I felt so small there. I came to understand how spiritual things go on in the world, not just at Maher. There were Fathers and Buddhist nuns, and many more. Every day

---

[41] "Beta" is loosely equivalent to dear one and is used with children.

RISING TO NEW LIFE

there were teachings from different faiths and religions. More than I ever knew. My heart felt all the spiritual energy there—I could feel it!

From there, Mangesh, another Maher boy, and I went to Maine, New Hampshire, Vermont, Nebraska and more states to tell people in the U.S. about Maher. This was both for fundraising and for us to learn about the U.S. [42]

Then we went to Seattle. First, we were counselors at a "Peace Camp" organized by a U.S. woman, Gretchen-Auntie, who also knows Maher. We did two weeks at Peace Camp as counselors, then a one week at "Hope Camp" on Whidbey Island, near Seattle, where I was a camper. Then we returned to Peace Camp as counselors again. It was interesting to experience both how it feels to be a camper and a counselor. It was challenging to be a counselor and to manage the children. They ranged in ages from six to fourteen. Because it was international, they came from many places, like Somalia and Syria. In India it is really easy to handle the children, even twenty children, but in the U.S. it was harder. It was harder due to different

---

[42] Author's note—I met Soni as host for her first stop in the U.S. She was hesitant and shy and not at all confident in her English. Now barely one year later she has blossomed! She is full of joy, life and light, and her English is wonderful! She is expressing complex ideas and feelings to me as she tells me her full story for this book.

Stories from Maher

rules and regulations plus I could feel how very different the cultures were. We had lots of fun. We taught them Bollywood dance and other activities, and we learned some activities from the campers as well. There was lots of love from them too!

Then I participated in the Gender Reconciliation workshop with Will-Uncle and Cynthia-Auntie. I was so shocked. Here in India so many girls and women do not speak of their problems. But here we were speaking these hard things, like abuse. It's really hard to share these things, but they made the space safe to share, for the women and men.

I was surprised to learn American women had troubles and abuse. I did not think they would have problems. But who would know that—of course they also have problems. But we don't know because we are not in their life and living their experiences. It was a powerful experience for me.

Didi reminds us to believe in prayer. Prayer has a huge positive energy and it surrounds us. I pray for all people—all the people in the world who are helping Maher. We don't know how many people are helping because they are so many! But I pray for all of them. There is a somewhat mysterious energy in the Maher prayer.

One time, my friend from college was really sad and telling me her problems. I asked her if she prayed. She said no; no one in her home prays. I thought: oh I am

RISING TO NEW LIFE

so lucky I got this in Maher! I told her how to pray and shared an interfaith prayer. Now she is practicing this! She told me thank you Soni so much for sharing this with me! I told her about Maher and she came to visit.

Because of Didi, I helped my friend. Didi is the light. She is the main candle to light the light in other hearts like mine. This way we are making a huge light in the world.

Maher is always helping others so I am always thinking about this—how can I help others?

I will get a job after university. (I have one more year after this). I am not thinking too much about the future. Didi teaches us to stay present. Though I have a dream to become a translator: Marathi and/or Hindi to English. I would like to learn Spanish too. I love languages: studying languages, I can stay up all night and not get tired. It's not like that with business courses or even dance.

Note: Soni has since completed her undergraduate degree and just took admission for an M.B.A.

Stories from Maher

From Unvalued Girl-child to MSW: Padmini's Story

I came to Maher when I was six years old, along with my two sisters. My father wanted a boy. He refused to support my sisters and I because we were girls. My mother had no other alternative but to look for support and care for her daughters. My mother brought all three of us to Pune. After we arrived there, she came to know about Maher. She brought my sisters and I to Maher to seek our admission.

At Maher I was able to go to school and participate in many of the Maher programs and activities. Dance became my passion. In 2007, I was part of the group who went to the U.K. to present dance and drama performances. I continued studying Kathak Indian Classical Dance (a storytelling dance) and I passed many levels of dance tests. I was part of Maher's Kathak Indian Classical Dance team. We represented Maher on many occasions. We also traveled to Mumbai and to other states in India to perform.

I completed a special diploma in education in college and worked for two years in a school to gain experience. But I always had a desire to work as Sister Lucy works for the world. I next completed my Bachelor of Arts and after that I completed a Master's in Social Work. I am also pursuing my Visharad (graduation) in Indian Kathak Classical Dance.

RISING TO NEW LIFE

I am now a member of Maher Society Team.[43] I work at Maher as a social worker. I dream of starting my own dance academy to spread healing through dance.

I am grateful for Didi and my Maher family for this wonderful and life changing opportunity that is Maher. Later this year I will marry another Maher boy, Gaus, and we will continue to work for Maher's mission together. Gaus is from a Muslim family while I am from a Hindu family, so this is an interfaith marriage. Sister Lucy traveled to visit my family and helped them to see beyond caste and religion and to understand what is in my and Gaus's hearts. Thanks to Maher, we have the blessings of both of our families.

From a Boy Washing Cars to Leader at Maher: Gaus's Story

This story is combined from multiple conversations this author had with Gaus, and an autobiographical story he wrote some years ago.

Gaus' parents worked at Weikfield Company. Two elder sisters also lived at home. Then his father had a stroke; he became paralyzed and bedridden. His mother took a second night job in a hospital, but there was no

---

[43] In Maharashtra state an NGO must have a set of no more than eleven Trustees and also a "Society." The Society can have many people and their role is to keep an eye on the Trustees and the work of the NGO.

Stories from Maher

longer enough money to send Gaus to school, even though he was clever. Even with his mother working two jobs, Gaus had to go to work too. He started working in a garage. His teachers offered to pay his school fees, but it was not enough: the family needed his income. He took a second job washing dishes nights behind a restaurant. This way he could sometimes bring home extra food to his family.

One day, a Maher social worker saw Gaus washing cars and asked why he was not in school. She asked to meet his parents. She and Sister Lucy went to Gaus' home to meet his family. Sister Lucy told his mother about Maher, and that they could help the family with food and medicines if Gaus left to come live at Maher and complete his education. All agreed and Gaus came to live at Maher. He was eight years old.

Gaus wrote:

I remember one vehicle came to my house. Didi and one lady got out from the vehicle and entered my house. I was so happy: I thought they were rich people brining some food for us. Didi talked with my mother.

Then Didi came to me and looked into my eyes. She asked only one question and this question changed my entire life. She asked me "School Janna chahoge" ("Do you want to go School?") and immediately I said "Yesssss!" I didn't know who she was or why she came to my house or anything about her. But I trusted her

RISING TO NEW LIFE

and I said yes. God sent an angel to my family.

That night I came to Maher. What I remember about my first day is that I got toothpaste for the first time and it tasted so good! I was given my own school uniform. I was so excited I slept holding tight to my uniform. And even better, I got a hot meal three times a day!

Through all my schooling, including completing my MBA, I lived with my Maher family. Maher gave me not only academic opportunities but also non-academic opportunities to improve myself.

Gaus returned to school, caught up, and quickly began winning awards. He was chosen "best actor" in the eighth standard. Later he was selected for Maharashtra Social Forum, a government education program for promising children from poor families. Gaus and another Maher girl both went on to Mumbai and then were selected to continue to the Forum's national competition in Delhi. Gaus won first place and was chosen to go to an International Forum in South Africa, but could not get a passport in time. Sister Lucy advised him not to be sad, that something else would come along. And it did— the trip to the U.K. to perform dance and drama. Gaus has since performed dance across India, U.S. and Europe.

Along with his Maher peers, Gaus emceed many big and small cultural events in Maher, including organizing the annual Sports Camp for 660-plus Maher

Stories from Maher

children. He organized values-based education seminars for Maher children, staff and the kindergarten teachers. He participated in a Non-Violent Communication (NVC) leadership Program in Pune.

Gaus attended B.J.S. College, winning Best Student Award for the year 2011-2012. In 2012 he received the Youth Excellence Award in Thought and Action by Kapoor Foundation, Canada. In 2016 he was chosen to be one of fifty university students from thousands across India to spend a month with the prime minister of India.

In addition to the above travel to U.K, Gaus travelled, first with Sister Lucy, then later with Mangesh, to many countries to represent Maher, including Germany, Austria, Italy, Belgium, Netherland, Scotland, and U.S.A. In 2013, he was a youth speaker in the "Dawn of Inter-Spirituality" conference in Washington state. He was a participant and then counselor for an "International Peace Camp" held in Seattle, Washington. Next, he completed an internship with PamTen in the U.S. After completing his MBA in International Business, Gaus was hired by PamTen in Hyderabad as a Human Resource professional. After one year, Gaus returned to Maher and began a full-time role in Human Resource Management at Maher. He is also learning all parts of Maher's operations, including establishing new centers.

RISING TO NEW LIFE

Gaus wrote of his dreams:

Didi was always teaching us to see big dreams for ourselves. She told us if we see only small dreams, it's a crime. So that's why I see the biggest dream of my life that I want become the President of India. And also to become a spiritual-motivational trainer[44] so I can give back to society and the world.

Finally, my dream is to become a resource person for Maher and to take Maher forward. I wish for a promising career ahead and to become a responsible person.

Dreams fulfilled (based on 3-2021 phone call with Gaus)

Gaus has been in Andhra Pradesh for the last two and a half months opening the new Maher center there. He is getting things set up, hiring and teaching staff (and later residents) "the Maher way," including the Maher values. He is working on government licenses, community relations, all of it! He went there with just one other from Pune, Asha, a Maher housemother of twenty years. There are thirty-five residents already. Just this week, Gaus rescued two women from the streets.

Andhra Pradesh is a state in southeastern India. The local language is Telugu, so none of the Maher staff

---

[44] While in Hyderabad, Gaus began giving these motivational talks as a side-job!

Stories from Maher

from Pune, including Gaus, speak the local language. Hindi[45] and English are the only options when hiring, training, talking with new residents, local community, etc. Of course, the professional staff, such as a local Andhra Pradesh MSW hired to oversee the center, speak English. So Gaus communicates with those only speaking Telugu with expressions, sounds, arm-waving ... and his heart.

Dancing in the streets: trust-building

One day Gaus saw a woman, seven months pregnant, living on the street. In true Maher fashion, he stopped the vehicle and sought to help her. They had no common language ... how could he help her trust him? At first she threw small rocks from the roadside at him, to make him go away. He spent four hours with her, to gain her trust. At one point he didn't know what to do—so he started dancing in the street! (Gaus is a very talented dancer.) The woman started to smile then to laugh. Gaus imagined her thinking "He's the crazy one—not me!" She eventually saw his joy and love

---

[45] While Hindi is the official national language of India, most Indians, outside a couple of northern states where it is regularly spoken, do not know Hindi. The local government schools in Andhra Pradesh, and most other states, teach only that state's local language. Therefore, generally the people seeking refuge will only speak their local language and dialect. This is a huge challenge in India.

RISING TO NEW LIFE

and was able to trust him enough to go with him to Maher. After arriving, the local staff could welcome her and explain where she was.

Gaus said "Someone helped me, so now I pay it forward. That is how the world works."

So far, this new Home is only for women. Gaus said he misses the children. One day, Gaus saw some children playing and so he wanted to engage with the children. The people there said "Oh no! Don't—they are Untouchables—you can't touch them!" Gaus was horrified. He went back to the new Maher center and got a bunch of snacks. He returned and gave out the treats and hugged every single one of those children!

This is Maher values in action: love all and exclude none, regardless of caste, gender, or religion. [This author is grinning, thinking, this community has no idea how their lives will change from Maher's presence!]

Hire a cook, hire a family

Gaus hired a new cook for the Home. He asked the cook about his family. The cook said he had only his mother and she is now home alone. Gaus told him "Don't leave her alone—bring her here! She can live here too and help the women!" She came. She is helping with the cooking and so happy. The cook was astonished! He said to Gaus "How do you even think to do things like this?! Working at Maher is so different

Stories from Maher

from any job I have ever known!" Gaus told him simply this is the Maher way.

Living the lessons of Maher

Later in our conversation, Gaus told me more about how he decides difficult questions. "Prayer is when you tell the Divine your troubles, your questions. Meditation is when you listen to what the Divine says to you." Prayer and meditation are his guides—and of course Sister Lucy!

Several weeks later, Gaus returned to Pune for his "Maher-brother" Yogesh's wedding to Poonam, another Maher young woman. Gaus will continue to travel to Andhra Pradesh to support the development of this new center. He says he has been a boy for so long, now he is learning responsibility. He is teaching and training people older than him, and they are happy to learn from him. He is so genuine, so charming, so full of joy. Everyone knows he comes from his heart. And that is Maher's way.

India's future is brighter

Gaus, and indeed all the young people in this chapter plus many more, is Maher's legacy. In this way, the work of Maher will go on even after Sister Lucy is gone. The work and the values will continue to spread to other parts of India. Maher has grown from a presence

RISING TO NEW LIFE

in five states to eight in just the last ten months, during COVID. Each center opened based on invitations from local people, donations of buildings, funds, and local support, and not based on any "grand plan" of Maher.

Chapter 8: Sister Lucy's Story

"There is a realization one day, and then you take one step. And then once you take that one step, you realize that you can't stop because whatever you've seen propels you into taking your second step, and the third step, and the fourth step."

– Leymah Gbowee[46]

"How Does Sister Lucy Do What She Does?"

This chapter is based on the author's conversations and travels with Sister Lucy over about ten years. It is one attempt to answer this question. I have written in Sister Lucy's voice so you the reader feel you are listening to some of these wonderful conversations and stories.

I was fourteen years old when I first saw poverty in the slums of Mumbai. I knew then, in my heart, that I wanted to become a nun and work to help the poor and destitute. At first my family disagreed. My parents

---

[46] 2011 Nobel Peace Laureate Leymah Gbowee is a Liberian peace activist, trained social worker, and women's rights advocate.

Rising to New Life

wanted me to complete my education first. They were worried about my future and my safety. But they saw my determination and gave in. I joined the Sisters of the Holy Cross.

I trained, took my vows and became a nun. I worked for the Sisters for many years, mostly in the kitchen. I rose to positions of responsibility as I was a very hard worker. After some time, I felt I wasn't doing enough for the poor—I wanted to work directly with the people. I asked to be transferred to work for Sister Noelline doing community work at Hope House outside Pune. I worked hard here and became very close to Sister Noelline. When I was with her at Hope House, I worked to sell the products that the women made in our workshops. I was not very happy and wanted to do more for the poorest of the poor.

Then one fateful day, a pregnant woman came to our gates seeking shelter. She believed her husband was about to murder her and she was very frightened. I believed her, but I had no authority to offer her (or any lay person) shelter and Sister Noelline was not there. I asked her to come back the next day.

That evening I heard screams and a great commotion in the village beyond our gates. I ran out to see what was happening. The woman recognized me and ran towards me: she was fully on fire. Her husband had thrown kerosene on her and set her on fire. We put out the flames and I begged someone to help me

Stories from Maher

transport her to the hospital. Finally one rickshaw driver agreed. When we got to the hospital it was already too late: she was dead. I asked the doctor if he could do anything for her unborn baby, but the baby too was fully burned to death.

I was devastated. I had no courage to question the existing system. She died because I could not give her shelter, because I followed the rules. This made me question everything even more deeply. I spent a lot of time alone in contemplation. I realized I also felt like I did not have the opportunity to give the message of Jesus to people. It was restricting my movements to be only inside the wall of the convent. I wanted to somehow go into the people. I didn't feel very comfortable inside walls. I did not need the walls to support me to live my vowed life. I felt I was strong enough. I did not want to project myself as a nun with a habit. I always felt my life should tell people who I am, rather than my habit.

So that was one of the reasons that living and working only inside the convent didn't make any sense to me. When things do not make sense to me, it's very difficult for me to follow. I cannot close my eyes and just follow someone. I may not fight or argue or even ask questions. That is not my way. I have to be convinced to do something. Once I am convinced, I am fully there. When I am not convinced, I sit quietly, with a straight face, and then I move on. But when I am

RISING TO NEW LIFE

convinced—then I act! That's it.

While I was wrestling with all this, the nuns could see my personality changing. I was still often joyful, but suddenly I got very irritated by small issues. They sent me for counseling with our priest, Father D'Sa.[47] He counseled me during this time and helped give me courage.

I vowed that what happened that night would never happen again. I had to be out with the people and able to offer shelter to these women. I had no idea what I would do. I had no money. I had no training or formal education for this sort of thing. But I really could not do anything else but try my best. I was afraid but determined.

Father D'Sa connected me to an Austrian man who felt compelled to do something for women in India. This man funded the first purchase of land in Vadhu Budruk village and part of the construction of the first building.

Very quickly we were overflowing. I was the only staff. And it wasn't only women who came—women fled with their children, all seeking shelter. I hadn't planned for this—though I should have—of course women flee with their children! But I am a nun, so I didn't think of this. Sometimes one woman came with three, or four, even five children! Everyone needed shelter, food, and clothing. The children needed to go to school. Often the

---

[47] Father D'Sa is a Franciscan Priest associated with the convent. He later served as a Maher Trustee for twenty-four years.

Stories from Maher

women did not know about hygiene or other basics. For example, most did not know how to prepare vegetables, only rice and dal. Vegetables are too expensive for so many of the poor people. Additionally, many of the women needed help to recover from trauma. I took care of everyone. I barely ever slept.

Then I hired Anand, and a year later, Hira, two wonderful social workers. They are both still with me.

About Interfaith and Caste

My faith has always sustained me. Over the years, between the teachings of my mother at home, exemplars at the convent including Sister Noelline, and counseling from Father D'Sa, I had developed a deep, resilient personal relationship with God, with Jesus as my heart's guide. I had a very clear set of values that guided me, rather than any "schooling" or "rulebook" on how to start an NGO.

I had some ideas of how things had to be. First, the people in these surrounding villages were mostly Hindu and a few Muslims, so what we did here must be interfaith. I have always drawn great strength and hope and courage from my faith, so I knew they would need this too, from their own faith. This is the biggest reason why the Church did not support me at all; they wanted and expected me to fail. Similarly, I felt all castes must be equally welcome and respected at Maher. Girl

RISING TO NEW LIFE

children must have the same educational opportunities as boys. So many elements of culture I was challenging, and more as we went on! (Such as widows remarrying, hygiene and modern plumbing.) This was very challenging. I had to make it up as I went along how to do this. Very few understood me, let alone supported me in this. I always wanted my life to be living and working with those in need; I did not want to be separated. It has not been an easy life, but Divine grace helped me with everything.

I kept in my mind from the very beginning: Maher was not for any particular religion or caste. So from the beginning I took people from different faiths to be the trustees and to be staff. This helped a lot to build up this interfaith aspect of Maher.

The Church I had to struggle with. My congregant I had to struggle with. They believed I had left the Church and the teachings. Plus, I had to struggle with other communities: they thought that since I am Christian and a Catholic that I had come to convert them.

Though the teachings of Jesus are deep within me, I dislike some of the church practices. Such as when we have the Mass and communion, we cannot give this to people of other religions. I don't like those kinds of things. But Christ's teachings—these are deep in my heart. I always ask myself: "If Jesus was here what would He do?" Because He did not have Christians, he just broke the bread and gave it to all the people who

214

Stories from Maher

were there. So from where did this "only for Catholics" come? I am not a scholar in the church or anything like that. I could not argue with any of the people who were coming here and questioning me. But at the same time my deep feeling inside me told me "It's not correct." So I moved away from Church practices like that.

I kept this in mind with every house that we named. Even "Maher," which means mother's home or mother's lap, I chose this name because it is non-denominational. Same with all the Homes, Projects, even Kindergartens: we chose Indian names, but purposely chose ones not of any particular caste or class or religion. Instead, names were perhaps a flower, or something that is meaningful, like Snebhavan, which means "Home of Love" or Suk Sandhya which means "At the End of the Day." Like that we named things, meaningful words that are appropriate for that home. Not any Saints, or Indian deities, or anything like that. This is something else the people of the Church could not accept.

Of course, the prayers we use—we pray only to the divine energy, not to any specific God. This also was intentional right from the beginning.

When children are born here, if the mother is there, she will name her baby. Otherwise, if we name the baby, we give a name that can belong to all religions. Like in my family: "Lily" "Rani" "Sibbi" ... these names are not from any caste or religion. Somehow from that time in my childhood, my family, the consciousness came.

Then of course when I became a nun it was very traditional. In the nunnery I did not consciously decide to disagree but neither did I agree. But if I had a personal choice, I would name something non-denominationally. Living and working with Sister Noelline and the local people also helped me to respect all. I didn't read a lot. However, I did read the books, and listened to recordings, of Anthony de Mello speaking about "the fearless religion." This also helped solidify my feelings about interfaith, even before I started Maher.

Jesus had all these people following him. He didn't talk about what religion they were—they must have been Jews, but also people of other religions. He was so comfortable to live in the home of the tax collector, and he was comfortable with anybody, even the poorest of the poor, for that matter. I felt my life should be something like that.

One example. We went to a Temple and we were given "prasad."[48] So when they gave it to me, I was going to eat it. Next to me was a Catholic priest and he smacked it away from me so it was flung to the floor. The Temple priest was watching this. I was so angry

---

[48] It is customary as you leave a Hindu temple, to be offered "prasad" usually a small sweet, nuts, or sometimes a small bowl of rice. Prasad is often translated as a love-offering.

with the Catholic priest. So I went a second time and got my prasad and I went to the side and ate it. The Temple priest did not fight. I was so happy. He didn't even ask me what was up, he just gave me the second prasad. When I went back to my group, the Catholic priest was so strongly angry with me. He accused me that I believed in paganism because I ate that! He was so upset with me! To me that sweet was a sweet and nothing else and it was offered in love. I asked him if he could see beyond the word prasad and see "love." He dismissed this idea saying that it's not love, they just cook it up and offer it to anybody. I said ok, but it's only for people who come to the Temple, so it is offered in love. They had a choice to do it or not do it. So they do it in love.

Now, with all the religious violence in India and the world, interfaith is an even more focal part of Maher's mission. How can families be secure when they are at war with their neighbors?

Challenges, Lessons, and Wisdom

After I started Maher, that first year I took everything personally. When the women told their stories I used to cry. I found this was not helping. It was a negative way of doing things, getting affected by all these stories. So after one year, when Hira came in, for three months we didn't take any new admissions. I handed over the

RISING TO NEW LIFE

project to Hira, and I went away for some serious counseling to know what was going on within me and also how to get into a strong spirituality more than praying. That did help me a lot.

It's not that I couldn't handle it; it's that I knew there was a better way to handle it. In my head I knew listening to their stories should not affect me, but there were sometimes where I could not manage. But I said no, the situation is there. I should have control over myself in all this. It should not affect me. This pain is her pain, but it should not have a negative effect on me because then I will only destroy myself. I was very convinced of this. But still, everything said and done, it was coming into me sometimes. You know, anger towards the man—like I wanted to really "finish him"— that kind of anger. That kind of thing. Then I said no, no, no; this is an actual situation and I must learn how to manage all this.

I went in for counseling and I shared all this. The counselor was fantastic. Now he lives in Ireland, he married an Irish woman, but he had really studied and he knew all about psychology, he had studied in America. So he could really help me out. He helped me to do what I wanted to do. He gave me tools; he helped me to understand myself much better. I won't say he did magic, but I really worked on myself with what he gave me. This helped me.

Consciously what I do—I say ok this is one more

Stories from Maher

problem, how do I cross this bridge now too? That kind of attitude I have. It's not that I don't feel, sometimes it turns my stomach inside a bit, but I say—ok.... now I am one step ahead: I can look at that man in an empathetic way, not in a judgmental way. It's not that every time I succeed. Like just now I am dealing with one rape case... yes, you feel the anger inside you, but I deal with it in a much more mature way.

I think the experiences of the women and the spiritual energy—it helps me a lot. As I said, I like to be alone sometimes, and I pray a lot. Not that I recite prayers, but I keep myself connected to the beautiful energy that is there. I take that in, that energy comes into me. And let the other go away. And sometimes even consciously I say, "let this go away." Even sometimes I see myself verbalizing it to myself: "Let this go now—it's too much. Let it go." I speak to myself sometimes.

Lessons from My Family

I give a lot of credit to my parents who brought me up in such a beautiful manner. I am very very happy with what they offered me. Not the worldly wealth, but the spiritual values that I had in my home, the family values I had in my home. These were very high. Inside me I am very strong, so nothing can destroy me inside.

My mother taught me also how to "find my center."

Rising to New Life

She said, "Problems will always be there, but we should not change ourselves as per the problem." We know who we are. She used to call everything Jesus, because she knew only that. She used to say "Connect with Jesus. Be with Jesus. Pray often." Consciously she put so much faith into us.

My mother was my first teacher. One day I was seven and playing happily. My mother was working in the garden. Our family was known to share rice with people who had no food. A beggar could come to our home with a bowl and they would be given a handful of raw rice. So this day a beggar woman came and my mother called me to get a handful of rice to share. I was annoyed to be interrupted from my play, like any seven-year-old. I huffed off, grabbed a handful of rice and tossed it carelessly in the woman's bowl and ran back to play.

My mother called me back and asked the beggar woman to wait. The woman said it's alright—she's just a child. She understood. But my mother wanted me to learn an important lesson.

She told me to go back and get another handful of rice, to put it in the woman's bowl with care, scolding me that I threw the rice the first time. My mother continued: whenever you give rice or something to any woman, any beggar, you must look into her eyes and see Jesus in her. And then she told me to apologize to that beggar woman; she told me to say "sorry."

Stories from Maher

I looked into the woman's eyes and while I don't remember what I saw then, I do remember my ego felt that so much! I have to say sorry to a beggar?! Oh my! That experience went not only into my brain but right into me!

Our mother also made my siblings and I carry "tiffin boxes" of food for people who were ill or to the parish priest. (Mother specially made non-spicy food for the priest since he was Italian.)

My family helped me a lot. They helped me not to dwell on how bad the situation is, the negatives that are there, but find solutions to help this woman who is here, right now. What does she need, right now? How we might solve the negatives, the problems, that will come later. But right now, she needs this or that.

While this author was at Maher, a woman, Pavani, was brought by her dying mother. This young woman had been raped as a child, beaten by her husband with a pipe, then raped and beaten again in her home. She was literally terrified all the time. Her hair was matted and full of lice. She smelled awful. She couldn't really talk, she made sort of fearful whimpers. She was afraid to eat or drink. She cowered from staff, even the women. Sister Lucy went to her, smiled her "Sister Lucy smile" and began to hand-feed Pavani, literally using her own fingers in the customary Indian way to feed this frightened woman. The woman began to calm, ate some food, drank some water. Later she finally allowed two of the staff women to lead her off for a bath and clean clothing.

As I watched Sister Lucy with Pavani, I thought ahhh this is what Pavani can feel, even in her terrified, out-of-her-mind state: Lucy is looking into her eyes and seeing Jesus. No wonder she would only eat from Sister Lucy's hands that first day.

"Doing the Needful"

All this gives me courage to say and do very difficult things. Even to a man, a husband threatening his wife, sometimes I am very, very strong. Sometimes, you can't imagine what all I do! Sometimes I even slap that man who has come—if he needs it.

Sometimes if I need to do it for the woman, I might also slap her. Because now recently I have to do this to one woman, a housemother, who was creating hell. I called her to my room and I gave her two slaps. What she was doing, (she was married and had two children, girls) she was taking the mobile and connecting to some men from the outside who were not good. She was trying to make my big girls also to connect to those men. She was trying to encourage prostitution!

She had nowhere else to go, she has a bad background. Her sister doesn't want her. Her parents don't want her. Her husband has left her. Literally she

Stories from Maher

was on the streets. But because of her two girls—I don't want them to lose their mother—so I have taken her. But she was creating such a bad situation. Normally staff deal with it, but she was telling lots of lies. I confiscated her mobile, so she is not accessible to the men, so then her "boyfriend" started calling on the Maher phone night and day. Staff told me all this: there were eighty calls for one day!

At first, she was denying everything. But staff and the big girls were telling me the truth. I said these girls will not lie to me. I talked to each girl one on one to be sure. And still she kept saying—no, I didn't do that. Then I called one of our staff who knew how to get the phone numbers out of her mobile. I found out who each person/number was, getting all the evidence. When some of them were not picking up, I called from her phone pretending to be her. Things like that. It took a long time, almost four hours, to get the whole truth out.

It was after we had the whole story, that is when I called her in to my room and gave her two slaps. "Will you stop it?! Or will you leave here? You have only those two choices. Either you stop, give up the mobile, and be here, and get into your head that you are wrong. Change your ways. Or get out with your two children and be on the street. The choice is yours."

I was not kind at all. But that turned her around. It worked so positively. She is changing, not everything of course. I was not angry. In your country it might not be ok to do this, but in my country it is ok. That turned her around. Today this morning she even came to thank me. She thanked me for doing that. She said "I was in an unconscious mind I think and you woke me up from somewhere."

I said no. You are still bluffing me. I cannot believe you that you have changed completely. (She wanted the phone, you see.) I said no, you have changed many things, but you have not changed fully. You need to ... otherwise you need to leave here. I know she cannot go. There is only one way; that she will be sleeping on the street.

In the beginning I could not have done that! Because being brought up in a very tender way in my home, I could not have done this, if I had not learned these techniques here. And I don't have the book knowledge, just the practical knowledge of dealing with people. I would have been an utter failure to run an organization if I did not have that common sense which my parents offered me.

Common sense and my mother's example are also what allows me also to have great patience with people, and to believe the best of them. Here is one more story:

Stories from Maher

Woman lied to save her daughter

A woman came with a girl child, saying it was her sister's daughter. Her sister had died and the father is irresponsible. She said she didn't have her sister's death certificate. This is common—in India the poor people just burn or bury their dead and they don't have a death certificate. I believed her and I admitted the child to Maher.

Soon I noticed that the child was always asking "When will my mother come?" I told her: you are referring to the woman as mother but that was your auntie who brought you. The girl said no, that was my mother.

I got a little confused. I asked her: When did your mother die?

She told me strongly that her mother did not die!

I showed her the records where it is written that her mother died. She said no, the one who brought me is my mother. Again, she says this. I was still confused but not wanting to upset the child, I said no more.

The next time the mother came, she explained that she made the girl call her "mother" because she did not want her to feel she is an orphan. I trusted this was true.

As the girl continued to grow up, I noticed she looked more and more like the one who brought her.

The next time the woman came, I took her aside and I said: There is no problem just tell me the truth. Tell me. The affection between the two was just like a mother and daughter.

Once Hira and I went to visit this family. Luckily for us the lady who admitted the child was not there. We asked the neighbor—how is this lady, how is the family? This neighbor told us the eldest daughter is in the project Maher. Two sons live here with her. (I did know this since she often brought the sons when she came to visit the daughter.)

The next time the lady came to visit, I told her: I have a feeling there is some untruth. Can you tell me? There is no problem, even if you told me lies before.

Then she confessed. She said yes, this is my real daughter.

I asked her, "Why did you put her in Maher and why did you tell lies?"

She said she had two things in mind. She did not want her daughter to be illiterate, like her. But her husband would not allow the daughter to go to school, only the sons. Then he said, "My daughter is a pretty looking girl." She didn't like the way her husband was looking at her daughter; she was afraid he would rape her. My daughter would be unable to protect herself because she is too small, she told me. She knew she would be safe at Maher and so that is why she sent her. She feared that if she told me the child had both a mother and a father, then Maher would not take the child. She lied to protect her daughter.

Stories from Maher

The girl stayed at Maher until she completed higher schooling. Then the mother told the girl what was what and how to protect herself. Then she brought her home. Also by this time the husband grew out of this weakness.

I don't call them liars. There is a reason they are lying. Find out that reason. We need to go beyond the lies, use our inner eye to look into that person. This way you can see the mother's love.

Looking to the Future

I look ahead to an India where there is no more need for places like Maher, because all of our people have all they need to live a good life. I know this work must continue on after me. I see the greatest hope for all of us in the children. I look at the children who have grown up here at Maher, some working out in the world, some who have come back to carry Maher forward. And I look at some of the staff who have worked here for many years, helping to build Maher to what it is today. I am so proud of all of them. They are living examples of what love can accomplish.

Chapter 9: How You Can Help

Maher's children say, "Thank you!"

I once heard Sister Lucy comforting a Western guest overwhelmed by the vast human suffering and need in India. Sister Lucy said "Even God can't alleviate all suffering. So I know I can't either. I just keep trying, I do my best. I keep learning."

Maher relies 100% on donations to meet its entire budget. Small donations to large generous bequests all make a significant difference. Maher is continually expanding as requests pour in from around India to "Come build a Maher here!" More and more people are

Stories from Maher

in need whether due to COVID, climate disasters causing food shortages and homelessness, or religious and social unrest. Maher's work in the villages (also 100% based on donations) works to make villages more stable and self-sufficient so fewer need to flee to shelters. You can be a part of Maher's success.

All donations to Maher Ashram, India are graciously accepted. Sister Lucy wants all of Maher's friends and benefactors to know that all your donations are well utilized for the upliftment of the less fortunate ones.

Starfish Parable

A young woman is walking along the sea's edge after a large storm. Hundreds and hundreds of starfish have washed up on the beach and will die. She stops, picks one up, throws it back in the water; takes another step or two, picks up another and throws it back in the water, and so on. A man comes along and asks her why she is doing this. She can't possibly save all the starfish, he points out—it's a waste of time! She picks up another starfish. As she is throwing it back into the sea, she looks at it with a smile and says, "I made a difference to this one!"

Ways to Donate:

Donations from US or Europe funneled through local supporters:

US Donors wishing an IRS Tax Deduction
Please make your donation by check or online at:
US Maher Friends, Inc.
36 Kinsington Street
South Burlington, VT 05403
USA
https://www.usmaherfriends.org/donate/

Donors in Austria:
Kontonummer des Vereins:
MAHER Österreichisches Hilfsprojekt für Not
leidende Frauen und Kinder in Indien
Volksbank
Wien AG BLZ 43000
IBAN: AT644300042862586007
BIC: VBWIATW1

Donors in Germany:
fam.marling@t-online.de / G.Binder@t-online.de
Förderverein für Maher e.V.; Liebfrauengemeinde
Filderstadt .
Mr. Thomas Kilian
Mission Procurator Deutschen,
Konogstr 64,
90402 Nurnberg
GERMANY   (Email ID- kilian@jesuitenmission.de)

Stories from Maher

Donors in U.K.:

Friends of Maher (UK) payments can be made either by post or by online banking.

For personal donations we are able to claim Gift Aid tax refunds—please email *treasurer@fomuk.org.uk* for details and a Gift Aid Declaration form.

- Cheques should be made payable to Friends of Maher (UK)
- Postal payments should be sent to the Treasurer at:
Friends of Maher (UK)
8 Hudson View Tadcaster
North Yorkshire
LS24 8JE
For online payments our Bank details are as follows:
Bank name: Lloyds Bank plc
Sort code: 30-93-91
Account name: Friends of Maher (UK)
Account number: 02209348

Donations from outside India, direct-wire to Maher:

Maher Ashram
Account Name: Maher
Swift Code—SBININBB104
IFSC NO. SBIN0000691
Account No: 40050122249
Branch Code: 00691
Bank Name: State Bank of India
Address: FCRA Cell, 4th Floor, State Bank of India,
New Delhi Main Branch, 11, Sansad Marg, New Delhi—110001, India
https://maherashram.org/donate/

RISING TO NEW LIFE

Donations from within India:
Account Name: Maher
Account No. 034104000033202
IFSC NO: IBKL0000034
Bank Name: IDBI Bank
Address: IDBI Bank, Hermes waves, Ground Floor
Shop no. 3 and 4, S.no. 212 Final plot
No.59, Kalyani Nagar, Yerwada, Pune—411006
Maher Permanent Account No. (PAN) (Income Tax): AABTM1421G

Donation amounts and what that buys (just as an idea):
The cost of supporting one home Maher is about $1,600 US dollars or 120,000 Indian rupees.

A home with about twenty children would be $80 per month per child or 6000 Indian rupees.

Relief efforts: COVID, cyclones, and more, Maher responds in the moment to meet emergency needs far beyond their doors.

Stories from Maher

Sample needs and costs: (list is from September, 2021.) Meant only to offer an idea of what your donations support, beyond housing, food, clothing, medical and school fees, and staffing.

Sr. No.	Particulars	No. Of items	Appx.Cost Rupees	In Euros € @ 85 Approx.	In USD $ @ 72 Approx.	In GBP £ @ Rs.100/-
1	Chairs	200	180000	2118	2500	1800
2	Pendol (Readymade)	1	175000	2059	2431	1750
3	Four Wheelers	2	2200000	25882	30556	22000
4	Smart Panel	1	300000	3529	4167	3000
5	Printer with Scanner	1	17000	200	236	170
6	Grinding Flour Mill	1	95000	1118	1319	950
7	Celing Fan	15	30000	353	417	300
8	Mobile Phones (Android)	4	64000	753	889	640
9	Invertor & Batteries	2	240000	2824	3333	2400
10	Two Wheeler	1	95000	1118	1319	950

<u>Samples of rupee conversions in late 2021:</u>
(Note the conversion rate changes frequently; check for current rates in your own currencies.)
100 (US dollars) = 7442 Indian rupees
100 Euros = 8633 Indian rupees
100 British pounds = 10181 Indian rupees

10,000 INR (Indian rupees) is approximately:
136 USD
115 Euro
99 British pounds

Acknowledgments

First and foremost I am grateful for Sister Lucy coming into my life and my heart. I am grateful to her, Hira, and the wonderful staff at Maher for sharing these stories, answering questions, clarifying details, and more. I am grateful for the amazing residents of Maher, the women, children and men who make up the community where I have always felt surrounded by love and joy. Also, I am grateful for the young people, now adults, whom I have been gifted to know and with whom I remain virtually connected even when I am not at Maher.

Many others have helped shape and write this book. These include my mother, Linda Cunningham, who read every chapter and Patricia Freeman who went through early iterations and helped me become a better writer. Deborah Heller and Ann Sanders helped me see I had two books instead of one massive book. (Book two will focus on the village and tribal development work and founding new sites. Stay tuned!) Finally, gratitude to my wonderful editor Tom Holbrook of RiverRun Bookstore who did the official editing and layout, getting the book from my laptop into the world!

My heart has been immersed in these stories now for two years and is softer and sweeter because of holding and caring for all these amazing people (staff and residents). May your heart also feel blessed.

Appendix One:

Vision, Mission and Values of Maher

VISION FOR THE FUTURE

No matter who we are, we walk together toward wholeness. All have the opportunity for a decent life, dignity, and happiness irrespective of caste, gender, or religion. There is no longer any work for organizations such as Maher.

MISSION

- Develop and deliver services to address the root causes of violence and despair and their effects, so women, children, men, and families are healthy, happy, and self-reliant.
- Where possible, support family reunification, providing services as needed to support healthy and stable homes.
- When family reunification is not possible or desirable, provide safe and loving residential educational and developmental services for children and women.
- Enable sustainable communities by addressing

RISING TO NEW LIFE

economic, education, health, and environmental issues focusing on villages and slums.

VALUES

- Embracing all people of all faiths, regardless of caste, class, or ethnicity
- Spiritually infused interfaith daily life and operations
- Unconditional love and respect for all
- Social justice for all, regardless of caste, class, or gender
- Truth, transparency, and fairness in all interactions and in distribution of resources
- Reawakening our personal relationship with Mother Earth & treating her as Body of the Divine
- Lifelong learning and continual re-evaluation and change

Appendix Two:

The Genius of Maher: Seven Areas of Uniqueness

1. **Women healing women; children passing it on: together creating a new India.** All Maher housemothers and many of the other staff themselves sought refuge at Maher. They understand the harsh realities of many women's lives and can offer compassion beyond measure. Part of their healing comes from helping the next to arrive: being able to help others helps grow self-esteem, self-confidence and inner strength. Maher's children, as they become young adults, volunteer their time to teach other disadvantaged children dance, music, self-empowerment, nonviolence, and more. They are learning a whole new set of values which will guide them as adults creating a new future.

2. **Core values drive operations and leadership.** Without being beholden to any particular church, philosophy, or group, Maher overtly upholds universal spiritual values, including unconditional love and respect for all; social justice for all; and

truth, transparency, and fairness in all interactions. A values-based NGO is a living, breathing culture of core values shared among all employees and residents. This distinguishes Maher from the traditional institutional feel of other organizations which have a more machine-like business approach and which rely on authoritarian relationships, or adherence to one particular faith.

3. **Holistic individual development.** Maher's programs respond to the physical, social, mental, and spiritual needs of the people seeking refuge. All of the residents have opportunities to learn the skills and self-confidence to prepare them for independent lives in their communities, whether with family members or on their own. The women and children, even those deeply traumatized, are made whole through unlimited love, nutritious food, regular exercise, education, artistic expression, and leadership and human development training. Many of the children choose to go on to college and university with Maher's continuing support.

4. **Needs-based support for healthy family and village life.** Maher will intervene at the woman's

Stories from Maher

request to reunite families where this can be done, changing the fabric of family life for the better. Maher also works to re-knit the fabric of village life through village awareness meetings, classes on overcoming alcoholism, establishment of local self-help groups, and other projects, thereby bringing improved health, well-being, dignity, and opportunities for all. This in turn helps stabilize and lift up all the families. Maher staff act as resources and guides, rather than as bearers of "the one way."

5. **Small "home-like" living centers as part of a larger community.** The women and children live in small "homes," generally no more than thirty children and three to five housemothers, within the larger Maher community, so that children grow up in a family-like environment rather than in large, impersonal, "efficient" institutions. Each child is treated as a unique individual, lovingly supported and brought up as parents would their own children. Daily operations, family life, and discipline are all heart-centered.

6. **Addressing the roots of violence and despair.** While starting with a focus on women and children, Maher has developed organically to address a broad array of interrelated social

problems. Every one of Maher's now twenty-four programs has a community outreach and educational component to help respectfully challenge and bring change to traditional, cultural norms that engender violence and despair.

7. **Anticorruption**. Maher has done all this without surrendering to the corruption that is prevalent in Indian society, thereby demonstrating the value and courage needed to bring change to the corrupt system that so undermines Indian growth and sustainability.

Appendix Three: Map and List of All Maher Centers in India

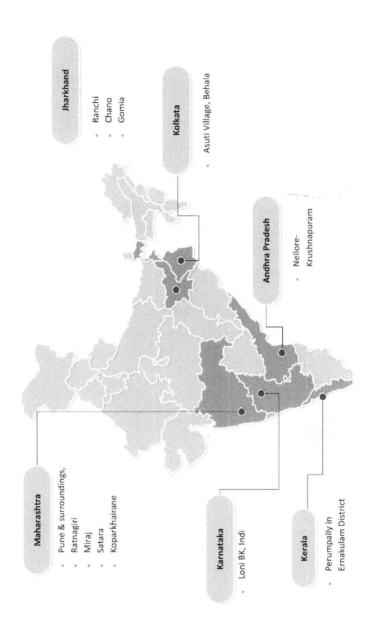

Appendix Four:

Additional Publications about Maher

Women Healing Women: A Model of Hope for Oppressed Women Everywhere
By Will Keepin, Ph.D. and Cynthia Brix, M.Div

Dignity from Despair: A Step By Step Guide for Transforming the Lives of Women and Children— Successful NGO Creation Using the Maher Model
By Darcy Cunningham, MBA

Beyond: An Encounter in Art
Edited by Wolfgang Schwaiger, Kristiane Petersmann, et al.

Made in United States
North Haven, CT
20 January 2022